# The Secret
## That's Holding
## You Back

T0165583

# The Secret That's Holding You Back

## Vincent Genna

MEDIA

**MEDIA**

Published 2022 by Gildan Media LLC
aka G&D Media
www.GandDmedia.com

Contact the author by email at believe@vincentgenna.com, and visit him at: vincentgenna.com, and LIKE him at: facebook.com/vincentgennamsw and facebook.com/the-secret-that's-holding-you-back

Front cover design by David Rheinhardt of Pyrographx

Interior design by Meghan Day Healey of Story Horse, LLC

Library of Congress Cataloging-in-Publication Data is available upon request

ISBN: 978-1-7225-0569-1

10   9   8   7   6   5   4   3   2   1

# Contents

# Introduction

The doorbell rang and my wife, Eileen, and I answered it together, giggling back at our living room full of guests like little school kids. Friends of ours had told us about a party they recently went to where a psychic was giving readings to the guests. They said everyone had a blast. I mean, what better innocent fun than a fortune-teller? We were a young couple as were our guests.

Eileen and I were both skeptical, but having that assurance from our friends, we contacted the psychic and set a date for our own party.

We opened the door and after congenially introducing ourselves, the first thing the psychic said was, "Wow. There's great energy coming from this home. The two of you have great energy." She sneaked her head in, looking at the kitchen and continued, "Oh, wow. You have a female Indian spirit hanging around in your kitchen. She's been letting you know she's here, hasn't she? Oh, I'm Doris."

That took Eileen and me by surprise because ever since we moved into that house we'd heard things banging around in the kitchen late at night. We chalked it up to old house sounds. Eileen and I were now intrigued.

One at a time, the guests went into the private room, laughing. "I can't wait to hear what she's going to say." They came out in amazement, stunned, saying, "I can't believe she just said that."

As each person exited the space, surprised and impressed about what Doris said, I was getting more excited because Doris seemed to be the real thing, and I knew she was going to tell me exciting news about my career. Eileen and I were the last two, and she wanted me to go before her. I made some tension-breaking joke before I walked in.

I sat on the other side of the card table, facing Doris and smiling from feeling a little awkward about what she might say. She asked for my hands, and I placed them in hers, but as soon as she held them, she immediately let go as if she had just been burned.

"Oh my God," she stammered emotionally. "I can't touch your hands. The soul of Jesus is around you and touching you. You're a very special soul."

She was speaking quickly, and I was unable to utter a sound. "In seven years you're going to become a great spiritual teacher, and Jesus is going to help you with the words to say all along the way." She paused.

In total shock and amazement, all I could say was, "What? Jesus is what?"

"He's touching your hands right now. I felt him on you. He's going to help you become a great spiritual teacher, and you're going to become very well known doing wonderful things for people and the world," she continued with great confidence and a gentle smile. She looked at me as if she were looking at Jesus and not me.

"Wait," I jammed in. "Do you see anything else about what I do now?" I didn't want to become a spiritual teacher. I mean, I believed in Jesus, though not the way the church did, and was glad he might be hanging around, but that's not what I wanted to hear.

"Well," she tried. "I see you're very creative and talented. But you're more than that. You're also very intuitive and psychic yourself. You have great powers you will be discovering. You're a performer of some kind now. I see you're going to be on TV."

Okay, now that's what I wanted to hear. "Now she's getting to the important stuff," I thought. "I'm a singer and actor now," I said.

"I see you have been on stage and in the movies. But I don't think you're going to keep doing that. You and your wife are very special souls and have been together in many past lifetimes. You will be traveling all around the world doing your work. And if you ever need help or guidance, call me." She ended the reading.

On one hand, I felt my heart drop from disappointment hearing about my career. On the other hand, I felt intrigued by what she was saying. I mean, who wouldn't when you're told you're powerful and Jesus is right by your side to help you? This was weird stuff.

"So what did she say?" Eileen asked as she was walking into the room for her reading.

"We'll talk about it when you come out, but apparently our lives will be changing like you can't believe."

Up until that fateful encounter, I thought I was meant to be a professional singer, actor, and dancer. I even landed a contract to be in the movie *Grease* with John Travolta and Olivia Newton John at age twenty-two. I didn't do it conventionally though. It went more like this:

"Hello, Pat (the choreographer). I know you chose me as the alternate male dancer in case one doesn't show up in Hollywood, but if I come out there on my own when rehearsal starts, would you get me on the set so I could be there if you need me for anything?" I boldly asked.

"Well, I could get you on the set," she said wearily, "but there's no guarantee I will even need you. I couldn't pay you anything, you know, and you could be wasting a lot of time waiting around," she argued.

"I don't care, Pat. It would be worth it to me to be there for you if you did need me. What do you say?"

"Okay, come to Hollywood, and I will have your name down at the Paramount Studio gate," she said. "I can't promise you anything."

As providence would have it, when I arrived for rehearsal, the choreographer informed me that Lorenzo Lamas, the Hollywood personality playing the jock, had a prior agreement and could not start rehearsing for three weeks. Since he was a crucial part of the gym scene dance contest, they needed a stand-in for him. And since I was already there, Pat asked if I would be willing to stand in, of course, without pay. I enthusiastically did.

Lorenzo arrived for the remaining rehearsals, so they no longer needed me. Once again, good fortune prevailed when Alan Carr, one of the producers, approached me one day while I was still there and offered me a role in the movie as a reward for my dedication and hard work. That led me to believe performing was my destiny, but six years later and my reading with psychic Doris completely transformed that belief.

Profound spiritual and supernatural events occurred directly after that evening, which changed my understanding of life, my attitudes, my persona, my beliefs, and, most of all, my purpose in life. I even discovered newly acquired psychic and mediumship skills to go along with all my other talents. My dreams and the passions shifted to those fueled by a compelling desire to be of help and service to others. Within the next two decades of my life, I became an internationally renowned psychic therapist, medium, and spiritual teacher. I fulfilled Doris's prophecy.

I have developed advanced psychic and medium skills not only to commune with human souls and spirits but also to communicate with dogs, cats, donkeys, horses, and gorillas, with dead people, and extraterrestrials. For almost four decades now, with these skills I've helped thousands of people around the world heal, unlock, and release their passions and purpose, and transform their lives through my inspiring radio and television interviews, dynamic and loving keynote presentations, workshops and classes, and private sessions. I offer my audiences and clients the opportunity for deep emotional healing and radical spiritual awakenings.

Everyone who experiences a Vincent Genna event or class goes home enlightened, energized, and empowered—emotionally prepared to unlock and release their passions and purposes and possessing the key to achieving their life goals and fulfilling their dreams.

This book is an accumulation of my years of study, research, and work in the fields of metaphysics, psychology, and spirituality, and my sixty-six years of life experience that includes empowering thousands of people from all over the world and different cultural backgrounds through my psychic medium sessions, media interviews, and lectures, and hearing innumerable incredible personal stories from the commonplace to the most severe.

I've combined the results of my studies and experience along with the knowledge and wisdom of past famous psychiatrists, psychologists, scientists, experts, spiritual leaders, authors, and luminaries to create a simple yet comprehensive understanding about how we stop ourselves from pursuing our passions and purposes, fulfilling our dreams, and creating the lives we desire and deserve unintentionally *and* intentionally all the time.

If you're *not* pursuing a rewarding career, if you're not in loving relationships, if you're not financially secure, if you're not healthy and vital, if you aren't fulfilling your purpose and passion, or don't even *know* your purpose or passion, then you're stopping yourself without even knowing it. There are mechanisms and processes at work in your psyche that your brain has unconsciously created that block and even sabotage your efforts to create a meaningful life. The bottom line is you don't believe what you think you believe!

We all know how it feels to feel and be less than authentic, less than fully self-expressed, less than feeling comfortable in our own skin. This book demonstrates how to develop the consciousness and practices to elevate your ability to live an authentically expressed life.

Find out why it's difficult to manifest what you desire in this life unless you follow the steps presented here. You may have the knowledge and information on how to use self-help, spiritual, and any other metaphysical principles, but there are specific psychological anomalies that you must become aware of to put *any* spiritual principles into working practice.

To illustrate the principles included in this book clearly, I've shared true stories of real clients and their real psychic and mediumship readings. Their names have been changed to maintain confidentiality. If someone reading this book has been to me for a reading, don't worry. You're not one of those stories . . . or are you?

Join the conversation and discover the secret on how you can become unstoppable!

# chapter 1

## You Know What You Don't Know?

$O$ne of my first clients was a woman who appeared to be in her forties. She attended the traveling psychic fair I was involved with in New Jersey. She chose me over the other nine psychics and mediums. I noticed she was attractive, personable, and smiling as she approached my table. She sat comfortably and introduced herself.

"Hello, Vincent. I'm Angie," she said pleasantly. "I chose you because something told me I needed to come to you. I'm very excited about this reading."

And before I could even say hello and instruct her about my process, she quickly continued to tell me she wanted to know all about her career. I immediately stopped her.

"I'm sorry, but please don't give me any personal details or information about you or your life. It's my job to connect with your soul and psychically tune in to all of that."

I also informed her that I would be telling her what she needed to hear, not what she wanted to hear. Angie agreed and sat back.

I shuffled my tarot deck, spread the cards across the table face down, had her choose ten random cards, and began her reading. (I used tarot cards in the beginning of my practice for both my client's and my comfort.)

After I laid out the cards she chose face up, I began, saying, "This is going to be a powerful reading, Angie. I already see that what you came here to get from this reading isn't as important as what you need to get. I'm considered the Big Leap psychic. I have an arrangement with the Universe to only bring to me those souls who are ready for big transformations, and since you're sitting in front of me, I don't care what inspired you to choose me, but apparently you're ready for huge changes in your life. Are you okay with this?"

"I am," she claimed. "Tell me everything you see."

That's what most of my clients tell me during their readings, though many times they're still shocked to hear what I have to say.

I had only twenty minutes to share with Angie all that I was seeing, so I went at it.

"I'm seeing three major scars on your heart from the loss of the love of a male. Two are from partners, lovers, right? One was from a boyfriend who broke up with you, and another is happening now. Isn't that right?"

"Yes."

"Wait, you're married?"

"Yes."

"And you're breaking up, getting a divorce?"

"We're separated right now."

"Well, that's two losses. I'm not seeing the third as a partner. Ah, it was your father. Did he leave or wasn't around while you were growing up?"

"No, he wasn't. He had to work a lot."

"Well, that's the third scar."

"But I knew he loved me," Angie interjected quickly.

"And as a child, how did you know that? When he was home, he didn't share his emotions much, right?"

"No. Dad didn't talk very much even when we saw him. And that wasn't very much because of all the hours he worked," she explained, and I let her continue since I had already tapped into that.

"I can tell you right now that as a child that bothered you, which is why I see it as a scar today. And Mom wasn't any more loving than Dad. In fact, I keep hearing critical words being thrown at you when you were young. That was from your mother, right?"

"Yes. Mom wasn't very nurturing, and she used to criticize everything I did. But I understood why because Dad wasn't around a lot, and Mom had to do all the work at home and take care of me and my brother," Angie defended.

"You're saying that at five and six and seven you had the wherewithal to understand why Mom wasn't giving you the love you were supposed to receive? Did you understand that about Dad too?" I asked. "Where was he when Mom was criticizing you? Did he protect you from her or give you any loving words to counter her negative ones?"

Angie thought about it for a moment and finally with a surprised, timid expression admitted, "No. I guess not."

"And that would have hurt you as a child, wouldn't it have?" I asked so she could herself make that connection with her genuine beliefs and not with her defensive ones.

Again, Angie responded with surprise as if to acknowledge this for the first time, "Yes, it would."

"I thought everything in my life was great," she said. "I thought I married a great man. I know he loved me and I love him. I don't understand what happened. I thought we were both very happy."

"None of what you just said is true," I interjected, "and you know it! I feel you have a strong intuition, but you're not listening to it. You knew when you first met your husband that he was not the right man, but you felt desperate for a companion, someone to fulfill your emotional needs, and as long as he gave you any positive attention, you married him. Isn't that true? And you can't lie to a psychic!"

"You're right, but I thought he would get better in time," she said. "And I was lonely."

"You also never thought you were good enough for anyone else. Isn't that correct too?" I added compassionately.

She nodded.

"With all of that going on in your life, you came here to ask me about your career?"

She said nothing.

"At least now your healing can begin."

I spent the rest of Angie's reading explaining how and why she harbored deep beliefs that she was unlovable and not good enough and that, because she is connected to a power, the Law of Attraction, those inner beliefs were manifesting her life outcomes, including her relationships and career. I presented Angie with the steps to completely transform her life. Though her reading was far deeper than she ever expected, she left feeling hopeful and most of all empowered with the knowledge of how to transform her life.

"Thank you so much. I never expected this. You've given me so much hope!" she gratefully expressed.

## The Evolution of the Environment-Made Mind

*Only 2 to 5 percent of the human mind is in conscious awareness.*
*That means 95 to 98 percent is in unawareness.*
*You have no idea what is going on in the majority of your mind.*

After all the years I studied and researched the body, mind, and spirit, as a metaphysician and psychotherapist, I've concluded the mind is divided into more areas of consciousness than the psychiatrists and psychologists labeled as the conscious, subconscious, and unconscious. Sigmund Freud had much to do with the discoveries of the unconscious mind. He, along with other psychiatrists, concluded all human innate knowing comes from the unconscious mind.

Carl Jung, one of Freud's better students, went on to further describe the unconscious mind and to include the superconscious mind, which is connected to a collective unconscious where all knowledge is housed. He also referred to this mind as the mind of God. This is actually the part of the mind where the soul's mind in connected. That's my theory where all our knowing comes from.

Now, my conjecture is that these new sections of the mind, with their own specific characteristics and functions, didn't develop until *after* we incarnated on Earth. When you're born into this world, you forget who you

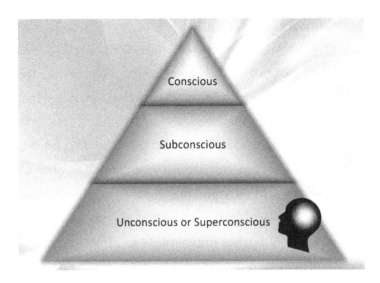

**The Three-Sectioned Mind Originated by Early Psychiatry With the Soul's Mind.**

are as an unlimited spiritual and divine being and who you were in your past lives just so you can create and live a whole new experience. You begin to grow up into a happy-go-lucky, innocent child filled with happiness and love, enjoying every moment, every taste, every color, every sound, every bug, every person, and wanting to share your melting ice cream cone with every stranger. And then, *bam*! Life happens to you, and you start to receive negative unconscious and conscious messages and influences from your environment. Those messages help to create your first set of thoughts, emotions, and beliefs.

We start to receive unconscious negative messages about ourselves quite early in life—sometimes even in utero. John Gray, author of *Men Are from Mars, Women Are from Venus*, in an earlier book, *What You Feel, You Can Heal*, wrote that self-love breaks down from the moment we receive the first unconscious message that we shouldn't appreciate ourselves.

Think about that for a moment. The very first unconscious message you can absorb energetically could be while you're still in your mommy's belly. That's true. There are plenty of studies that show playing calming or classical music during pregnancy can affect the infant positively while in utero and once born. If the fetus can be affected by positive external energy, can't it also be affected by negative? While you were developing in the womb, what could you have been absorbing if your parents were arguing about you being an unwanted pregnancy or if you were a pregnancy from an act of sexual violence? Can't that first unconscious negative message even come from Mom being disappointed that you turned out to be a boy instead of the girl she dreamed of having?

When you receive your first negative messages from your parents, siblings, other family members, teachers, or your environment, what happens next is due to protective mechanisms in your brain. From what I've seen and experienced, I believe our negative stories fracture our three-sectioned minds, and the brain creates a fourth section.

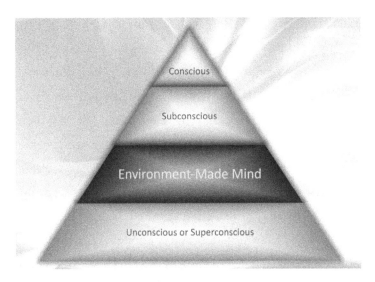

**New Four-Section Mind With Environment-Made Mind.**

Positive and negative thoughts and energy are like oil and vinegar; they don't mix. That's why they're opposite sides of a magnet, so the brain splits the mind to create a container for those new negative thoughts and feelings. I call this new container the Environment-Made Mind or EMM. I believe all our maladaptive beliefs about who we are and our relationship to our environment and to our lives are formed and held here.

As souls, we first come into the world with self-love. We can't help it. The Source we come from is made of love. However, the moment we receive our first negative message from our new world, there's a conflict between what we should be experiencing and what we're actually experiencing. For self-preservation, the brain needs to resolve all conflicts. Because our immature and egocentric minds can't reason, they can only come to one conclusion: "Something is wrong with me. They don't love me." Those are the first maladaptive beliefs we form. And it's that first set of self-beliefs, along with others that develop with every negative message we receive, that are harbored in the EMM.

I also refer to these beliefs as the I'm nots: "I'm not good enough," "I'm not smart enough," "I'm not beautiful enough," "I'm not deserving enough," "I'm not lovable," "I'm not whatever enough." It's in this mind where most of our emotional pains originate. In my reading for Angie, she formed her beliefs that she was unlovable and not good enough, and her brain held them in the EMM.

The brain forms the Environment-Made Mind for two primary reasons. First, because the unconscious or superconscious mind, as Carl Jung labeled it after Freud, houses the soul's mind and only knows of all God-given positive beliefs and feelings about us and the world. The soul's mind connects us with our intuition and can't coexist with negative beliefs and feelings.

The second reason the brain forms another section is, ironically, out of the need for survival. The brain comes with built-in protective mechanisms to assure our survival. The brain's survival tactic, then, is to hold onto all experiences, good and bad, just in case it may need them to reference someday.

Even though our maladaptive beliefs are destructive, the brain automatically keeps them. It would be so much easier to release those ridiculous beliefs and feelings if our brains didn't do that. And since they can't coexist with the soul's mind in the superconscious, the brain fractions off another section to retain those destructive maladaptive beliefs. I call this section the Environment-Made Mind because, when we are young, our minds are like sponges absorbing and taking everything in from our interactions with people and from the environment. Our youthful minds are just too underdeveloped to consciously create our own set of critical-thinking beliefs, so the environment helps to influence our immature concrete beliefs.

Then, the EMM holds all negative beliefs, while the superconscious and soul's mind holds all positive beliefs. And the superconscious and soul's mind are located below the EMM and deep within your psyche. Your EMM is now the closest mind to your subconscious, and therefore the major trainer of your subconscious mind's automatic thoughts, reactions, and beliefs, and the closest to your conscious mind. That is one of the reasons it's easier or faster to have a negative reaction and feeling before a positive one. Hypothetically, your superconscious *and* intuitive thoughts have further to travel considering the barrier of the Environment-Made Mind.

Do you ever wonder why your inner child's voice is so hard to quiet or forget, why you may have so many maladaptive beliefs about yourself, why you can't "move past your past" as so many practitioners suggest, and why that voice is so ingrained that it still influences you even today?

The negative messages we receive about ourselves start so early in our lives, and they don't always come from blatant abuse. Sometimes they're subtle, negative messages, and sometimes they're loud and harsh. Either way, they're the beliefs we start developing about ourselves because of the way our worlds treat us and respond to us. They can come from a teacher trying to make you a good student or a parent attempting to help you learn and grow up. But for the most part, our negative, maladaptive self-beliefs come from those who have a lot of their own negative and maladaptive self-beliefs.

Children translate the attention they receive or don't receive as whether they're lovable or not. Our lovability factor is primary to our existence as souls. We were created from love, we're made of love, so love is all we know within our soul mind. And we use love to measure everything about our evolvement and growth as beings. Positive attention equals we are lovable, and negative, or lack of attention, means we're not. That is the simplicity of children and what they need. Thus, it's not always about the verbal messages you may receive from the adults in your life. How did they all attend or not attend to you?

Maybe you're convinced you had a *Brady Bunch* life (you'll have to research that television show if you don't know it), but I can assure you, because of the world we have been living in for hundreds of years, there's no way you were unaffected by some family or environmental dysfunction or history. The reason the world is the way it is today is because of the domination of the Environment-Made Mind over the reasoning and intellectual minds. And that domination was perpetuated and passed down from generation to generation.

Don't get me wrong, positive thoughts and soulful feelings of love can squeeze through and make it to your consciousness, which is why you can experience moments of happiness, joy, love, and even self-confidence. However, those moments may not last long because the size and negative contents of your EMM will soon strangle the positive moments. The more your EMM becomes filled, the more problematic your life will become. And since your beliefs manifest your life, which I'll talk more about later, it becomes a never-ending spiral of bad experiences. The bad experiences produce negative self-thoughts and beliefs, which attract more bad experiences that produce more bad beliefs, and the cycle continues until you can disrupt it some way. Worse, however, I believe the EMM gave way to yet another fracture as your immature mind developed for the same preservation reason. This new section turns out to be the most destructive of all.

What maladaptive beliefs do you think are in your Environment-Made Mind? What could be getting in your way of attracting the right partner or any healthy relationship into your life? As with Angie, she had two failed love interests, and her hidden unlovable and not good enough self-beliefs manifested them. What are your hidden beliefs?

# chapter 2

## Losing Our Keys

Our stories define us; they shape us and scar us and sometimes build us up, like Angie's story did for her. They lead us to become who we are today. No matter how intense or ordinary our stories, they're guaranteed to cause us to completely lose our connection with the one key ability that will make everything we attempt become a reality. This ability that we all have isn't a unique or special gift. Each one of us received it innately upon creation, but unless we use it, nothing we try in life really works.

What is this ability? I'll get to it. But first, see if you identify with any of these situations and personality traits.

You're not happy like Angie in the previous chapter. In upcoming chapters, you'll meet Sean who was in an unfulfilling job. You'll examine your unstable financial status as I do with Tony and Frances. Maybe your health is less than vital and is controlled by genetic predispositions, mirroring Ellen's story, which you'll read about. Maybe you have given up on your dreams and passions or you don't have any dreams or passions at all, and you settle for whatever luckily comes into your life. Maybe you're saying, "Life isn't fair, and then you die." Maybe, instead, your life's better than others, but still you're aware of your unlived potential.

In an attempt to improve or transform the quality of your life, you read numerous self-help and spiritual books by some of the most inspirational and motivational gurus and greatest spiritual authors and scholars. With dedication, you study and apply ancient universal laws and principles that teach about your capacity as a spiritual being to be able to manifest and create the life you desire and deserve. You attend several master classes, retreats, and conferences that promise to inspire higher consciousness, wisdom, and knowledge. You even join a New Age or New Thought spiritual community of like-minded members preaching, practicing, and reinforcing all those past-demonstrated principles. And *still* you're left saying repeatedly, "God, it's not working." Why?

I present many ideologies, conceptions, philosophies, and theories throughout this book—some you may or may not have heard about or known before. I present my personal insights and the beliefs that form the foundation of my studies and research for the material I share here, starting with the Environment-Made Mind. To that end, then, while reading this book, you may be thinking to yourself that you already know everything I'm saying. Good for you then. However, forget all you think you know.

I finally began to see my dreams come to fruition when I proclaimed out loud, "Okay, I'm going to forget what I think I know to find out what I really know. I'm going to live like I'm ignorant of everything. No matter what I've learned over the past years of my studies, I'm going to forget it all. Since I'm not attaining all I want, that must mean I believe something not benefiting my highest good, or I don't believe something I should. After all, Albert Einstein said, and I paraphrase, you can't solve a problem with the same set of beliefs that created it. Show me the beliefs that are blocking me, Universe. Bring it on. I'm ready."

I encourage you to declare something similar. Set aside criticisms or any predispositions you may have so you can receive the benefits from this book. Read and reread everything here as if you're reading it for the first time. Have you ever gone to your favorite vacation spot like Disneyland more than one time? Each time you go, it's a new experience. And if you imagine each time you go as your first time there, it will be your very best time.

This may be the first time you're learning about the information in this book, so it may seem advanced. Then, again, you may be an expert on this material, and you may think it's simple. Let go of all judgments. Novice or scholar, if you were drawn to this book for any reason, chances are, one time or many, you've stopped or blocked yourself from creating the life you want. If that's the case, then I wrote this book just for you.

I can guarantee you will gain something from reading this book. If you commit yourself to working on the precepts I put forth here diligently, consistently, and with integrity, you'll have the chance to experience your greatest transformation to a higher consciousness where you're the master of your life and all your divinely endowed gifts.

I believe something greater than us caused our existence. We were created by a greater power, the energy source of all there is—The Light, Spirit, Yahweh, El-Shaddai, Jehovah, Elohim, Abba, Adonai, God, or whatever you wish to call it. Due to my Catholic upbringing, I refer to this omnipotent power as God. I believe the way God created us was by dividing part of itself to become each of us. Thus, created in God's image, each one of us has all of God's qualities, makeup, or DNA, shall we say.

To illustrate this, consider the human fertilized egg in the stage called the zygote.

At the zygote stage, the one cell begins to divide itself into the over 33 billion cells to form who we are going to be, and within each of those cells is a DNA strand that is the blueprint of our entire makeup. Scientifically, one DNA strand can form another you. Remember the cloned sheep in the 1980s? Scientists extracted DNA from one cell of a living sheep and, through a special laboratory-controlled biological process, cloned or duplicated the subject with all the same features and traits.

In theory, we each took the DNA of God that defines who we are and who God is. Hence, each one of us, upon creation, not only has God's qualities but we also have God's ability to co-create all we want. By inherent nature, then, we are all unlimited beings capable of creating unlimited love, happiness, wellness, fulfillment, and prosperity. That also means if you're not creating all you truly desire, something's not working, and somehow you're stopping yourself.

Maybe you're able to manifest some things but not others. That still means you're getting in your way of manifesting consistently. (And if you're already creating all you want and fulfilling your dreams and purpose, then you know what's working, and that's excellent. This book will then serve as a reinforcement and a validation to what you have already awakened within you.)

Is it possible that you can't create all you want and get the parts of your life working as promised because there isn't enough information about how to manifest and attract all you desire? At this point in history, I think not. Currently, there's an enormous wealth of wisdom and information at our fingertips. There have been so many positive enlightenment movements, be they spiritual or psychological, from personal self-growth and spiritual gurus and authors such as the Dalai Lama, Dr. Phil, Lao Tzu, Dr. Wayne Dyer, Louise Hay, Abraham Hicks, and even Oprah who have rewritten, reminded, and reexplained some of the most ancient wisdom and knowledge.

You may have been exposed to all the universal principles and teachings through writings such as *The Law of Attraction: The Basics of the Teachings of Abraham*, *Ask and It Is Given: Learning to Manifest Your Desires*, *The Power of Now: A Guide to Spiritual Enlightenment*, *The Power of Intention: Learning to Co-Create Your World Your Way*, and *The Secret*. All of these say the exact same message about us being magnificent beings and co-creators with God, capable of manifesting all we want.

Therefore, if it's not that there isn't enough knowledge, information, theories, principles, or concepts that claim we are attracting and manifesting beings, could it be all the so-called wisdom is bogus? That, too, can't be possible. This information is ancient and has been around for thousands of years because the scholars throughout time have been preserving what they've experienced to be the answers and truths about who we are as scribed by the earliest enlightened messengers and masters.

A plethora of evidence from those who have consciously manifested their greatest desires throughout our existence proves these ageless principles. Even contemporary scientists are turning to that ancient wisdom to reexplain the origin of humanity. Read *New York Times* bestselling New Age author and computer geologist Gregg Braden's book *Deep Truth: Igniting the Memory of Our Origin, History, Destiny, and Fate*, and you'll be shocked to learn how so much of the old theories of evolution are all scientifically being disproven. So, it's not the information that is causing the problem.

Maybe we aren't applying the information accurately, or it isn't being explained comprehensively. That's not a reasonable excuse either. Book publishing companies now average $2 billion in sales of self-help and spiritual books, videos, CDs, calendars, affirmation decks, angel card decks, novelties, how-to and spirituality-for-dummies-type book sales per year. Written by thousands of authors, though the information may be the same, each book is explained in a different way to appeal to any reader.

Again, that can't be the answer either. It's not the information itself or the lack of information that's not working, and it's not the application of the information. Yet, you still find yourself blocked and whispering, thinking, ruminating, masticating, enumerating, crying, and yelling in total frustration, "God, it's not working! What's stopping me?" Therefore, the answer has to be something else. Something you're doing or something you aren't doing, and actually it's both.

Up until this point, I've been discussing something you *are* doing that is keeping you from manifesting what you want: you've been stopping and sabotaging yourself with all those Environment-Made Mind and Adult-Made Mind beliefs and thoughts. Now let's discuss the most important part about becoming unstoppable—something you *aren't* doing.

Let me express it to you this way. When you want to bake a cake, you can use all wonderful organic ingredients and mix them all together using the best Rachael Ray utensils and mixing bowls just like a professional chef. Then pour the batter into the finest quality Pampered Chef stoneware baker and place it in the top-of-the-line Jenn Air oven. However, if you forget to do the most important thing first, you will never end up with a cake. What's the first line of instructions in all baking recipes? Preheat the oven. You have to turn on the heat. The heat processes all the ingredients into a cake.

To summarize, what I'm saying is this: If you're reading books, practicing principles, attending conferences, joining spiritual centers, listening to enlightening speakers, taking classes, meditating, eating organically, exercising, and still can't get anything to work the way all the self-help, spiritual, and metaphysical books and ancient writings say you can, then the bottom-line, miracle, bingo answer is you're not applying the main process.

What is this most key process that would make everything you attempt work? I can't tell you. Well, at least not now. This process is so simple and sounds almost trite to point it out, so I'm not going to disclose it yet. I first want to share more stories of psychic readings I have performed for others who were stopping themselves—in an attempt to explain through their trials and tribulations how you might lose track of the process.

Sometimes in order to heal or resolve a problem, you need to learn how you got the problem. If you walk into a doctor's office with a giant gash on your leg, before the doctor even begins to treat you, the first diagnostic question from the doctor is, "What happened? How did you get this gash?" Your answer leads the doctor to the correct healing course of treatment, right? Besides, if I tell you what you aren't doing right now, you'll predictably say, "Oh, I knew that," when, in fact, you actually didn't.

Let me introduce you to Sean.

chapter 3

## Defense Has the Ball

*I* had a client call me for a phone reading from London. His name was Sean and he had heard me on an interview on the *Coast-to-Coast AM* radio show with George Noory and had listened to me many times on my Unity online radio show. He booked an appointment for one hour. With his British accent, unlike my New York and North Carolina mixed accent, Sean sounded calm and pleasant. Right at the beginning, I gave him my usual instructions and told him how I work. I asked him if he had any questions before we started.

Right away he blurted out, "Yes, I do. I want to know what you see in my career."

"Sean, stop! Don't tell me what you want to know or give me any details about anything. I want to see what

I get first. Then you can ask those kinds of questions at the end if I don't happen to answer them during the reading. Okay?"

"Okay, sorry."

I began. "Well, you already brought up your career, so I might as well talk about that first, but then I also want to talk about a move and your health in that order."

"Okay."

"I feel a lot of stress and anxiety regarding work. A lot of unhappiness too. I mean a lot! Isn't that correct? Just answer yes or no."

"Yes."

"But it wasn't always like that. Correct?"

"That's right. I—"

"Stop! Remember don't give me any details. The anxiety and stress aren't just being felt by you. Your bosses are feeling that too. I'm getting a lot of loss around your work. Wait! Did your company lay off several people? Did you get laid off or furloughed because of the coronavirus?"

"Yes, I did. Laid off. And you're right. Several of us did. Can I just add something to that?" Sean requested before I could say anything.

"Go ahead."

"Unfortunately, they can't hire me back. The coronavirus really hurt them," he explained.

"And I know you have been looking and looking for another job and can't find one, can you?" I shared with a little sarcasm in my voice. I knew the answer, but I wanted Sean to say it.

"No, I can't find one."

"And do you know why you can't find one?" This was a redundant question because I knew he was going to come up with some excuse, but I was using this to eventually make a point with him.

"I do," he came back sounding frustrated. "It's because there's nothing out there for me. I'm fifty years old and no one wants to hire a fifty-year-old. Also, because of COVID-19, every company is having a difficult time. I even sent resumes to companies in the US and haven't heard anything. I'm not ready to retire and I need a job. Everyone is having a difficult time. The job market is quite harsh today."

"Um, I'm getting a lot of technical stuff around your job and lots of information. You have to be very left brained to do this work; you have to think a lot. Very high stressed, too, because people and the company depend on you to fix things for them. Also, computers. It's certainly not a touchy-feely job, is it? I'm seeing initials in my head for the job you have. And the only initials I know for a computer technical job are *i* and *t*. Your job is as an IT techie, isn't it," I interpreted.

"Yes, I am. I'm in IT, information technology," Sean replied.

"Oh, okay. I get the computers and technical and high-stress stuff. You fix computer and software issues when things aren't working right with them. I know my wife's company's IT person," I shared with Sean so he knew I understood the type of work he did.

I continued, "And that's what you have been applying for after you lost your job."

"Yes, everywhere," he added with more frustration.

"No wonder you're not getting any responses. You *hate* that work!" I said with great confidence and an excited voice.

"No, I don't," he argued back. "I was very good at my job. And at the time, it was very secure and well-paying."

"Being good at your job has nothing to do with liking your work," I said. "Being good at your job has more to do with your work ethics. And, Sean, you would do well at any job you had. Isn't that correct?"

"Yes. I always do my best," he shared as if he was feeling proud.

"Yes, you do. I know that. You did your best even when you were a kid in school and at home, didn't you, Sean? In fact, from the age of five when you first started school, didn't your parents, especially your father, expect you to do your best all the time?"

I was leading up to a point regarding what I was seeing in Sean's Environment-Made Mind.

"Yes, they always expected us to do our best. They wanted us to be successful in life. And, for the most part, me, my brother, and sister all did quite well in business."

"I'm curious, Sean. I'm getting that you're very creative and meant to use your right brain more than your left in business. Didn't you play an instrument when you were younger, Sean? A guitar, perhaps?"

Usually, when I ask questions it's not because I require an answer. I already know the answer. I asked with a tone to suggest I knew a secret of Sean's, which tends to stress the point of their answer.

"I did play the guitar in my teens and twenties but stopped," he said with laughter in his voice.

"And didn't you also enjoy writing stories and poems, Sean?" I knew what I was leading up to.

"I did, very much," he shared more solemnly.

"Why did you choose IT work, Sean?" I asked leading him.

"For a couple of reasons. I knew I could get a well-paying and secure position in IT. I did well in all my computer engineering courses at university, so I figured that was my field. Besides, my father thought that was a much more practical career for me to get into. Both my parents seemed very pleased with my choice as well as my work."

"So you received much approval and positive attention from them for doing this work?"

"Yes."

"What did they think of your guitar playing and writing, Sean?" I asked knowing this answer too. Sometimes it's necessary to be able to get the client to speak the answer rather than just confirm it. That's from my psychology training and experience. I use both psychic and psychotherapy techniques in my work.

"They didn't think very much about that at all. They just thought it was a child's hobby and activity," he answered correctly.

"Actually, I'm hearing they said it was silly to be writing poems and playing the guitar. Isn't that true, Sean?"

"As I remember, yes, they did say that at some time," he recalled with a little thought.

"So you're going to try to convince me that a totally right-brained, creative person like you would rather be working in a left-brain field?"

I wanted Sean to think deeper for his answer, so I continued. "Wait a minute. A spirit just stepped in. Male. He's showing me a picture of a room he is standing in. It looks like a boy's room, and there is a poster of some sort on the wall. It's very busy. I can hardly make out the details, but it looks like a picture of a concert, a rock concert, I guess. He's holding up a guitar. He's your father. Your father's deceased, Sean, isn't he? And that is your room he's showing me, isn't it?"

"Holy shit! Yes, it is! And that was a poster I had of a rock band playing at a concert. Dad's here?" he asked with great anticipation.

"He is. Not a very big man. Thin in stature, dark hair, average height. But there's a serious look on his face. It's not from what he is feeling today. It's from an actual time he came in your room and talked to you about your guitar playing. Apparently, he was ridiculing you for your interest in rock bands and playing the guitar. That's why he is showing me he's standing in front of the poster." I paused to let Sean respond to all that I saw.

"Yeah, he wasn't too keen about rock bands and their music. He was old fashioned that way. I remember that day. I was fourteen years old. You're freaking me out here." Sean sounded choked up.

"Well, right now he feels pretty bad about that. He's letting me feel his emotions, and he's sad because he feels he took that away from you. He's reaching out right now and giving you the guitar. He's saying to the best of what I hear, 'Please, play it again, Sean. I love you very much. I'm so proud of who you are and am so sorry.'" That was all his father wanted to say. I gave Sean time to process that because he became very quiet. I knew he was crying.

"Wow! Damn! That . . . uh . . . was quite . . . an experience. I've had other readings before, but my dad never came through like that. Tell him I forgave him a long time ago. I hope he's okay," Sean replied with concern.

"He can hear you without me. And he's okay. Remember, he's surrounded with loving beings there supporting and guiding him all the way. He'll resolve those sad feelings far quicker than you will get over yours." I went on to summarize what Sean had held inside.

"You never wanted to work in the IT industry, which, by the way, is the reason you lost your job. You didn't lose it. Your soul and the Universe took you out of it. And that's also the reason you're not being called for any of those jobs you applied for. You truly don't want any of them, so you manifested no callbacks. And another part of your mind, the most destructive part, blocked what you were really feeling and created a whole set of false beliefs and excuses as to why you were laid off and couldn't find new work."

I continued before letting him speak. "You're a writer, Sean. That's what I'm seeing. And a talented one. Your soul came into this world to inspire people with words. And you always wanted to do your best only because that is how you obtained love from your parents. That was the message you received from how they gave you attention. You interpreted their approval of your good work as 'They love me!' And you interpreted their lack of approval as 'They don't love me!' Of course, you would naturally strive for their approval to gain their love. Choosing a more practical career pleased your parents and, bingo, you got their love. Now, understand most of this was on an unconscious level, Sean. You didn't even know this was how you were believing and being influenced. You created a set of beliefs to hide and shield you from your real beliefs."

There was a long pause of silence, and I knew why. For the first time, Sean's defenses were weakened from my words. He was faced with his true feelings, including those painful "I'm not good enough" Environment-Made Mind ones.

My heart is always moved when I hear my clients cry because that means I broke through their defenses and touched something genuine inside them. This is especially true with a man because his defenses are harder to break through for the most part. Sean responded with gentle tears.

"You're right. I always wanted to write poems and lyrics. I only became a computer engineer to make my parents proud of me. And I never thought I was good enough to write or play the guitar. I still can't believe Dad came. I needed to hear that so badly." He barely was able to get his words out.

"Well, now's the time to start writing and start playing again. You need to honor your inner child and your desires. You're good enough and deserving enough. And remember, you certainly have the time now. You're not working," I added lightheartedly.

Sean laughed. I knew he was on a healing path once he acknowledged both his defenses and maladaptive inner beliefs. I finished the rest of his reading by giving him the steps he needed to continue on his new journey, and I encouraged him to stop stopping himself and gain control over his defense mechanisms and, finally, his negative self-beliefs.

## You Don't Believe What You Think You Believe

*When you think you know what you believe, you're wrong. You don't believe what you think you believe.*

Two of the primary functions of the human brain are to keep us alive and to protect us. From the moment we are born, our bodies create antigens and antibodies to protect us from most infections and diseases. The same is true for our minds. As our bodies develop, so do our mental protective mechanisms.

As negative influences from our environments infiltrate our thoughts consciously or unconsciously and create unpleasant, uncomfortable, and painful emotions and feelings, our brains begin to respond by kicking into protective mode. That protective mode becomes stronger and stronger as we reach puberty. Hormones increase constantly within our bodies, affecting not only our physical development but also our emotional development. The feelings of joy, happiness, and love intensify along with sadness, despair, and hurt. It's right around adolescence that our defense mechanisms begin to form—our emotional mind's protections.

Sigmund Freud discovered and labeled ten different defense mechanisms we begin to develop during our later teens that continue to gain strength during our young adult and adult years. You know, those famous defenses no one can ever name or remember: rationalization, intellectualization, projection, reaction formation, regression, repression, suppression, displacement, sublimation, and, of course, denial. By using these mechanisms, we create a new set of beliefs to protect and shield us from our original maladaptive and painful ones.

If you have done any reading about the human brain, along with what I stated earlier about the sectioning of the Environment-Made Mind (EMM), you'll understand how complex and completely organized the brain is. Each section of the mind plays a specific role in our survival. So when anything new is introduced into the brain that can't be integrated with an already developed and functional section, the brain develops a new section or pathway to accommodate the new input just as it did to create the EMM.

This new set of beliefs created by the brain to protect us from the painful constructs already in the EMM

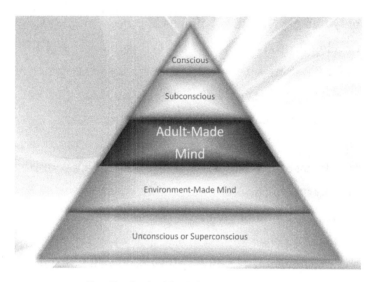

**New Five-Section Mind With Adult-Made Mind.**

can't be combined with the ones the EMM already houses because there would be utter chaos within that portion of the mind. Nor can the new set of defensive beliefs be assimilated in the superconscious and soul's mind. Therefore, the brain creates a new compartment or level of consciousness to contain the newly established defenses and beliefs. I call this new section the Adult-Made Mind or AMM. It's located directly above the EMM and just below the subconscious mind.

It's in this mind where we develop and harbor a new set of beliefs about who we are and about life based on what makes us feel better and as a shield against the EMM. Here, Sean created beliefs about why he wasn't able to get another job: "It's because there's nothing out there for me," and "It's because of COVID-19." The Adult-Made Mind will construct any defense or excuse it deems necessary for self-protection, and this pushes the EMM with its painful beliefs deeper into our psyche to hide it from our conscious awareness.

It's in this mind that we also develop our prejudices and judgments of the world and others because it makes us feel better to judge and blame someone else instead of ourselves. The AMM creates such excuses as these: "I know why I didn't get that promotion. My boss is an ass." "My husband (or wife) totally abused me and controlled me, and that's why I was never able to do anything with my life." "Our lives and the economy suck today because of that Muslim, Black president we had." "Gays are causing all the natural disasters because they're an abomination to God."

We also develop maladaptive physical behaviors, such as addictions, due to the AMM wanting to self-medicate and distract us from our pain. Substance abuse is the most common one. The degree of strength and control the AMM has over us directly correlates to the degree of pain we feel from the EMM. The AMM helps us survive and cope in life, but it totally blocks and stops who we really are and our true abilities that are held in the soul's and superconscious mind. The Adult-Made

Mind gets us in trouble the most. You've heard this mind more commonly referred to as the "wall of protection" we build or the masks we hide behind.

Since the AMM is now closest to your subconscious and conscious minds, it has the greatest influence over you. All along, the beliefs in your EMM still try to jam their way up to the subconscious and conscious minds, and occasionally make it there. Some people's AMMs are so weak, they hear nothing but the beliefs from their EMMs and go through life consciously thinking and saying self-demeaning thoughts. Meanwhile, in the depths of your mind, beneath your EMM and AMM, is your soul's mind desperately trying to sneak the truths to your consciousness. Sometimes they make it and you receive intuitive and inspirational insights, but at other times your AMM stops your soul's thoughts and pushes them way back down because the AMM thinks the EMM is trying to break through with all the negative beliefs that are going to cause you harm.

In that case, you will do things like talk yourself out of an inspiration or intuition because you don't trust it—just like Angie did in my first story. She first felt in her gut that the man she was about to marry was wrong for her, but her AMM talked her out of it. Your left-brain thinking taps into your AMM belief systems while your right-brain feeling taps into your soul's innate wisdom.

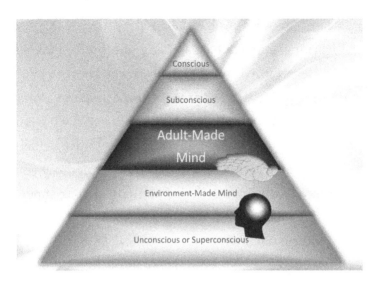

The Adult-Made Mind Suppressing the Environment-Made Mind *and* Soul's Mind.

Carl Rogers, a contemporary psychologist who created the area of psychology called humanist psychology, proposed that if you remove all the social constraints from humans, we would all naturally move in the direction of happiness, fulfillment, and well-being—always. These two minds, the Environment-Made Mind and Adult-Made Mind, are the constraints he was referring to.

For the most part, most of us are living by the control of our EMMs, the AMMs, and subconscious and conscious minds, with an occasional influence from our soul's mind. And because of our powers to convince ourselves of anything, we believe everything in the AMM is real and the truth. Oh, people are convinced they believe what they think they believe.

Here's another problem caused by the AMM. All the learning, applications, and attempts you're making to create better lives are being processed through your AMM. However, you *can't* process from fake minds. Your EMM and AMM minds hold falsehoods about who you are, so when you're attempting to apply positive principles and practices, and they don't work, it's because you processed them in your AMM and not in your superconscious and soul's mind.

Another way of understanding this concept is when you say something like, "I understand it intellectually, but I can't feel it in my heart." Not only does your AMM block the good messages coming up from deep within your psyche and soul, but it also blocks them going down as well.

One positive benefit of having the AMM: it blocks anything new from entering your EMM, good and bad. Therefore, once the AMM develops, you can't add new maladaptive beliefs to your EMM. You can only compound and embellish those that are already in there. The bottom line is this: due to your mind fracturing and creating the Adult-Made Mind, *you don't believe what you think you believe.*

What Adult-Made Mind defenses do you think you created to protect yourself from your Environment-Made Mind beliefs? How strong are they? Don't even think about the maladaptive self-beliefs you may have; just

consider the defensive ones that have helped you cope
through your life. Sean had powerful AMM defenses.
Until he was fifty years old, he convinced himself that he
was supposed to be an IT engineer and that writing and
playing music were frivolous and a waste of time.

Maybe as you're reading this you're thinking, "He's
talking about someone else, not me," or "This is all crap.
I don't believe any of this." Those are AMM beliefs also.
Look at the way people are acting today all around
the world. All the fighting, lashing out, hatred, killing,
bigotry, racism, polarization, and political rhetoric is
caused by the workings of the AMM. Can you begin to
imagine what torments and pains those people may have
harbored in their EMMs for their AMMs to become so
strong? Are you one of those people?

Work backward with my concepts to help understand and maybe even develop compassion for yourself
and for those people.

- They have all these defenses that the brain created
  to shield and protect them from their painful self-
  beliefs held in their AMMs.

- And all their painful self-beliefs formed from the
  negative messages they received from their environments that are held in their EMMs.

- Finally, all the negative messages they received from
  their environments covered and blocked their souls'
  minds, which were always trying to remind them

how divine and magnificent they really were, but the soul mind could not get through the EMM, AMM, and subconscious mind to their conscious minds.

You could be doing the same thing. In fact, if you're not manifesting the life you desire, fulfilling your passions and purpose, or don't even know what your passions and purpose are, then, for sure, your AMM and EMM are stopping and sabotaging you.

# chapter 4

## The Force Is with You

*A*t the end of most of my readings, my clients ask if they can call me again for a follow-up reading. I tell everyone not to call me for at least three months or more unless some crisis occurs. It takes that long for the client's energy to change enough for me to be able to get new messages. Otherwise, I'm just repeating what I said at their last reading. Also, I don't want people depending on me for guidance.

The purpose of my readings is to connect clients to their souls and empower them to trust and depend on themselves for their own guidance. Everyone is connected to Source, Spirit, God, whatever you wish to call God and capable of tapping into that Source to get their best insight and answers. Most of my clients do return for more readings or mediumship connections, but that's usually after six months to a year. I have several clients who called me back after two years and a few even after five.

All my return clients claim their lives changed so much for the better after my readings with them. Some are in healthy and loving relationships now. Others went into more rewarding and fulfilling careers. Several of my clients wanted to do the work I do or something similar, and I told them they were meant to be healers and mystics themselves. They started their own businesses, which became quite successful.

A few times, I've discovered my past clients in one of my psychic and mediumship courses. I'm so moved and feel so blessed when I do hear back from any of my clients, and they tell me how much better their lives have become because of how I helped them. Of course, I always return that praise by saying, "I may have given you all the tools you needed, but you did all the work! Take credit for that."

I've allowed a few clients to turn to me more while they're making major transitions in their lives because they have no other support network. However, I continue to empower them to depend on their internal guidance. One client in particular, Maria, comes to mind.

Maria called for her appointment, and immediately after I said hello, she quickly and anxiously exclaimed, "Oh, my God, I'm so looking forward to this reading with you. I'm fifty-five and my life has been filled with nothing but torment and grief. Every one of my family and friends betrayed me. Even my old boyfriends and everyone I meet betray and abuse me. I can't trust anyone. And I'm very ill from arthritis and other diseases. The doctors don't know what to do for me. I'm so concerned about my finances because I basically can't work anymore due to my illness. I saw you at an event, and I know you can help me. I've nowhere else to turn!"

She didn't pause for a breath, so I didn't have a chance to jump in and instruct her not to give me any details. She did my job for me and gave me all the information I would have liked to intuit myself. At this point I realized this was going to be more psychic and spiritual *therapy,* and hopefully mediumship connections, than giving vocation or purpose directions. Besides, all my red flags went up. *Is Maria going to become dependent on me?*

Whenever someone tells me, "Everyone betrays and torments me," and "The doctors don't know what to do for me," my psychotherapy instincts ignite, and I hear my trained mind warn, "Paranoia or delusions psychosis," though I don't conclude that instantly. I only prepare myself to refer the client to a professional therapist if necessary. I had earned my professional certification as a Licensed Clinical Social Worker (LCSW) several years ago but not today. That's not the work I wish to do anymore. However, I felt my soul and Spirit tell me I could help Maria and that she was already seeing a psychotherapist.

"Slow down, Maria, and take a deep breath," I was finally able to interject. "Try not to give me any other details. I want to connect with your soul myself and clairvoyantly see your life. And you're safe now, so relax. You can trust me!"

"Oh, I'm so sorry. I didn't know," she apologized.

"It's okay. Everybody does that." My past experience with anxious psychotherapy clients helped me calm and comfort Maria, so I could tune in better. I told her my process and I jumped right into the reading.

"Obviously, from what you already told me, I know there's a lot of anxiety and turmoil in your life. But I see that all coming from a very scarred past, from childhood. With just a yes or no, is that correct?"

"Yes!"

Focusing on my inner voice, I shared what I was hearing. "Your father drank a lot when you were younger. Isn't that correct?"

"Yes!"

"I hear a lot of mean and abusive things he said to you. Isn't that correct?"

"Yes!"

"Your mother was ill when you were younger. She had . . . cancer. Isn't that correct?"

"Yes!"

"Pancreatic, correct?"

"That's right!"

"You were nine or ten years old, weren't you?"

"Oh, my God! Yes, I was."

"She died when you were ten, didn't she?" I share this as thoughtfully as I could.

"Yes, she did! Oh, I miss my mama," she said and began to cry.

"She just came in. Your mother is here with us now. She was a beautiful woman who always took care of her appearance when she was alive, didn't she?"

"Mama was very beautiful. Please tell her hello." Maria perked up a bit at this point.

"You can tell her. She hears you."

"I miss you, Mom," Maria cried out.

"She says she misses you, too, but is around you all the time. She is telling me she is so sorry your father threw away your dolls. Even the one she bought you when you both went shopping one day. Mom just said you gave the doll a special name. Um, she's showing me an image to try to get me the name . . . um . . . oh, wait! Is that a picture of the *Wizard of Oz* she's showing me? That's one of my favorite movies, and she's using what's in my head. Dorothy? Dorothy, that's the name you gave the doll because you loved that movie."

"Oh, wow! Yes, I loved that movie as a little girl, and I always wanted to be Dorothy. Yes, I named that dolly

Dorothy. You remember that, Mom. I remember that day you got me that doll, Mom. And yes, Dad did; he did. He threw away Dorothy. He was so mean. He became so mean to me, especially after you died, Mom," she said, clearly upset.

I continued to share her mother's words and pieces of evidence her mother was giving me. "Your mother is showing me a beautiful stone or crystal pendant necklace that was hers that she wanted you to have, but your sister took it. It looks blue. Isn't that true?"

"Yes, oh, yes! My sister is a bitch, and she knew Mom wanted me to have it, but she took it. I'm still mad at her! Will I ever get that back?" Maria asked me and her mother.

"Your mom is saying it doesn't matter; don't think about that anymore. Your mom wants me to go on with what I see."

"Oh, okay. Bye, Mom," Maria cried out.

"No, she's still here. She just wants me to continue. I'm seeing four love scars on your heart. One from your father emotionally abandoning you. One from your mom dying. One from a broken love partnership, a divorce, and one you have just experienced with a boyfriend. I know the first two are correct. The last two are correct, too, aren't they?"

"Yes. I was married and then got a divorce because he betrayed me and slept with another woman, and I just broke up with my boyfriend because he started abusing me mentally. He was always trying to make me feel like I was nuts."

"Well, you shouldn't have been with him or the first guy, and you know it. Isn't that correct," I came back at her right away.

"Yes, I know. They were bad for me, but I was desperate. Everything bad keeps happening to me, and I keep attracting the worst people into my life, and I don't know why. That's why I made an appointment with you."

"Well, I think you do know why, but you don't know you know why, which is also why you don't know what to do to stop it!"

She laughed and said, "Okay, so what do I know about why bad things keep happening to me?"

"Maria, you're ingrained with the beliefs that there's something wrong with you, that you're unlovable and not good enough. Your mother died, which you took as abandonment even if you knew she was sick. Then your father and sister abused you, and none of your other family members supported you. That's more abandonment and rejection. There's an unconscious, innate knowing within everyone about love. The younger you are, the stronger the knowing. The messages from the environment either validate or conflict with that knowing. If the messages are negative, as yours were, the brain must resolve the conflict between the unconscious knowing you should be loved and this doesn't feel like love. And because children are all egocentric when first are born into this world, the only answer a child can come up with to resolve the conflict is, 'It must be me. I'm unlovable. I'm not good enough.' That's enough for any kid to believe he or she is broken, that something is wrong with them. Children blame themselves for everything that happens with or without knowing it."

I continued. "Now here's the problem with those beliefs. It's those beliefs that keep influencing what you're manifesting in your life. You know about the Law of Attraction?"

"I do. I read about that and saw programs about it."

"Good. Then you understand that because you have the beliefs you're unlovable and not good enough, you keep manifesting all that stuff you don't want in your life, including attracting all the wrong people. The good thing is, as long as you understand you're manifesting all that, you can start manifesting what you *do* want in your life."

"Oh, wow! I can?" she asked hopefully.

I continued the session by answering all of Maria's questions, and there were many: "Should I leave the job I'm working at?" "Should I look for another boyfriend?" "Will I ever find the right guy who will treat me right?" "Will my finances ever get better?" "Will I get my health back?" And more. By the end of the session, Maria was extremely grateful.

"Thank you so much for all your help. I understand what I need to do. I'm sure I will be calling you again," she excitedly expressed.

"Don't call me too soon. You need to learn to depend on yourself and get your own messages. I gave you an exercise to be able to do that. Commit to yourself and the work of healing yourself. There's nothing wrong with you, only with what you've been taught to believe about yourself. Change those beliefs and you will change everything."

## Beliefs Create Life

Thoughts do not create. Beliefs do.
You must believe it into being.

Not every unconscious or conscious negative message from the environment is obvious or as intense as Maria's were. Some people's stories are ordinary, and some are even more tragic than hers. Many people tell me during a psychic session after sharing what I saw deep in their EMMs (Environment-Made Minds), "I don't remember experiencing anything bad in my childhood." They say, "I feel I had a happy childhood," or "My family was wonderful." Yet, no matter what they do to create the lives they want, they keep running into dead ends. I see what they can't see, what's deeply entrenched and hidden in their psyches.

As a child, your immature mind couldn't fill in the blanks or interpret anything other than what was concrete. Also, since the concept of love is ambiguous, the amount and type of attention you received as a child was how you translated your lovability factor. So, even while Daddy was home and you got along well with him, the amount of time he spent at work could have still greatly affected you negatively. "Where's Daddy? When is he coming home?" When you asked those questions, you didn't ask with the expectation of hearing an answer you could intellectualize. You were actually questioning, "Why isn't Daddy here to play with me? Doesn't Daddy love me?"

Depending on your sensitivity level and temperament at that time, the lack of Daddy's presence could have been received as an unconscious negative message from your environment. If that was your first negative message, then that's the exact moment your EMM formed. This is only one example of how you can receive and perceive messages negatively.

I can actually write a full book listing the types of negative messages we receive from our young worlds. Your maladaptive dogma continues to form from conception to about twenty-three years old, depending on how slowly you mature. Even in your mother's womb, you're sensing the outer world and absorbing the good and bad energy that you're subjected to. Were there fights about your mother becoming pregnant, or regular arguments or violence around Mom while you were still a mere fetus? Those first twenty-three years of your life is a long time to develop and hold onto beliefs that are intimidating, relentless, cruel, obstinate, frightening, sabotaging, punishing, condemning, disparaging, and a host of other painful adjectives.

As I said earlier, the average person wants to believe his or her childhood was wonderful with loving and attentive parents. I mean, who wouldn't? But the reality is human issues along with individual and family dysfunction have been passed down from generation to generation throughout the ages, to the point of calling it normal. I promise you, if you were drawn to read this book, your childhood *was* normal, which is what the problem is.

Then second, and the bottom line is this: if you don't have what you want and deserve in your life right now, if you lack anywhere in your life—in a rewarding vocation, fulfilling relationships, love, financial freedom, and perfect health—then you're harboring unconscious EMM beliefs that are stopping you from creating what you want and causing you to perpetuate what you don't want. It works this way whether you agree or disagree with this understanding. These parts of your mind don't function under your command or approval and disapproval. It is what it is, and you are what you are. And you're magnificent. You just forgot that.

While we're talking about creating and manifesting, let me speak on those subjects more comprehensively, so we're all on the same page so to speak. At this point I need to talk about the spiritual aspect of who we are. After all, we are all composed of body, mind, and spirit, which makes us more than just physical beings. If you truly want to become unstoppable, here's where you need to expand your beliefs. I'm not talking about your religious beliefs. I'm talking about developing your spiritual ones—what is your relationship with yourself, others, the world, and some deity or greater force? Religion was man's way of interpreting those beliefs and putting them into practice.

No matter what religious belief system you practice, God, Yahweh, Jehovah, Allah, Buddha, Brahma, or whatever you call the creator created us. Even if you don't believe in a "God" creator, you still need to trust that we come from some higher force and that somehow we are connected to it to manifest the life you want. And that power or force permeates everything and is everywhere.

If you can't believe at least that much, then you have completely stopped the chance of evolving into the highest being you can be and becoming unstoppable.

George Lucas based his entire movie saga, *Star Wars,* around the concept of that "Force" and that everyone is tapped into it, some more than others, but all can learn to use it. That's not a fantasy or sci-fi idea. It's real and it has a name: the Law of Attraction.

The Law of Attraction is one of the primordial universal laws God created at the beginning of the universe. And just like the laws of gravity, aerodynamics, karma, and others, the Law of Attraction works deliberately by your intentional use of it or automatically by your unintentional use. It's working all the time. We are using the Law of Attraction during every moment of our lives even while sleeping. It's the God-source, universal power that is constantly on and never depleted. As such, it's most beneficial that you know the dynamics of both the Law of Attraction and manifesting because, again, if you wish to stop stopping yourself and create the life you deserve, then these are principles you must know and be able to command.

For your purpose, being aware of how the Law of Attraction really works not only will give you conscious control and use of it, but knowing it also will support my previous theories of the EMM beliefs you're harboring and how they're constantly influencing your experiences whether you know it or not.

Putting this all together, you're manifesting your life moment to moment, consciously or unconsciously.

This is so important to understand that I have to spell it out as clearly as I can here. If you're trying to create what you *want* using any or all the spiritual, metaphysical, or self-help principles and practices you might have learned, and nothing you're doing is working, and you manifest moment to moment consciously or unconsciously, then the only deductive conclusion you can come to is you're creating everything you *don't* want. Simply, if you're not creating into your reality what you want, then you're creating what you don't want all the time even while you sleep. How? From the beliefs in your EMM.

We already established that the Law of Attraction force is everywhere. Supposedly, we control it from our thoughts by means of the manifesting process. Every book written on the Law of Attraction stresses that repeatedly. They all say, "It's all about your thoughts." *Ask and It Is Given: Learning to Manifest Your Desires* and *The Law of Attraction* by Esther and Jerry Hicks are excellent books where you can read more about steps and procedures of manifesting. Just know that following those steps isn't enough without the vital process I'm writing about. The principles put forth in books like those are just like some of the wonderful ingredients you need to collect to bake a delicious cake but not what is going to turn them into that nonfattening, seven-layer, chocolate fudge cake you want. Remember, Maria said she had done a lot of work, but terrible things were still happening to her.

The law states that as you think, so you are—that your thoughts manifest your life. However, it's a slight misguidance to say the Law of Attraction and manifesting works by your thoughts and that you can *think* something into existence. That's actually not accurate. Thoughts do not create. Beliefs do. You have to believe it into being. The Law of Attraction and manifesting works solely from our beliefs. And since this is a "law" we're talking about, there are no exceptions.

Let me acknowledge, though, that your conscious thoughts influence your beliefs, but so do your unconscious ones. Ever since the dawn of the New Age movement, which publicly brought to light these ancient understandings of the Law of Attraction, people have been trying to apply them studiously with limited or no success. That's because they've been taught that they manifest with their conscious thoughts. Change your thoughts and you change your outcome. That is the exact premise for the New Thought spiritual movement and teachings: to have a "new life," you need to have "new thoughts." In truth, it should be called the New Belief movement.

It's not with your thoughts you manifest. It's with your beliefs. And you don't create with your conscious beliefs; you manifest with your subconscious and

unconscious beliefs. That's profoundly the most important feature of the Law of Attraction and manifesting.

Think about it. If we did manifest from our conscious beliefs and thoughts, we'd immediately bring
something into existence the moment we thought something. If that was the case, think of the hazards. How
many times would everyone be winning the lottery?
Worse yet, how many times out of frustration have you
said to yourself, "I'm a jackass," or told someone to "drop
dead," or better yet, "Go f*#k yourself"? That visualization is blinding me. Sure, you can laugh at the examples,
but seriously think about the repercussions. We'd never
survive nor evolve with that type of ability. Hence, the
power resides in our unaware minds.

This is all good even if we do create from deep within
the mind since that is where our soul's mind resides. And
the soul is directly connected to the mind of God and
all its qualities, so what could go wrong? What mind did
I say is wedged between your superconscious and subconscious minds? Right. Your EMM, Environment-Made
Mind. What could go wrong is your EMM can block
good beliefs trying to come up from your soul's mind.
The result is we're using the greatest power we have, the
Law of Attraction through the process of manifesting,
with our EMM beliefs instead of our God-given beliefs.

That's why, if we're not creating what we want,
we're creating what we don't want. The soul inspires

us regarding what to want because it holds the truth of what we can have. However, the beliefs we need to manifest those desires into your reality are being influenced by and coming from our EMM beliefs instead of from our soul's truths. The bottom line: we manifest from our unconscious core beliefs, and since our EMM beliefs are the closest to our conscious awareness, which may be why we tend to focus on the negative rather than positive, they have the greater control on our core beliefs.

Here's an example using Maria's case of how the Law of Attraction works and what basically happens between the conscious and Environment-Made Minds. You can substitute Maria's example with any one of yours.

"I would really love a boyfriend I can trust and who will love me in return. I deserve a good man!" Maria declares consciously one day. Her desires and thoughts begin an energy-building process. Her genuine and intense desire builds up the energy even more and is getting ready to be released into the universal law to find *and* attract that boyfriend who is out there somewhere among the billions of men in the world. Then just when Maria's energy, filled with desire, is about to be released, her EMM instantaneously and unconsciously jumps in and interjects, "But I'm not lovable. Nobody cares for me anyway. Why should I get anyone who's going to treat me well?" Those beliefs were in there from her childhood experiences.

Dang! Now, with her negative self-beliefs mixed in with her best desires and hopes, that energy is released into the Universe, and, lo and behold, Maria meets another guy who eventually uses, abuses, and denigrates her. Maybe not right away because she had to wait for the courtship phase of dating, where everyone is on their best behavior, to end. The result: Maria is left with feelings of disappointment and disillusionment in herself once again. And since she's read about the Law of Attraction and its claims, Maria's left with disappointment and disillusionment with that as well.

This is exactly how Maria kept attracting the wrong people and situations into her life. Maria's inner Environment-Made Mind beliefs took over her manifesting process instead of her hopeful conscious mind beliefs over and over again.

This is why I emphasize the importance of knowing everything about the EMM and the maladaptive or inner child beliefs it contains. Certainly, the purpose of this book is to teach you how to tap into that astonishing force and control it consciously and with the best intentions so you can stop stopping yourself and finally make everything work.

Look at your life now. How has it been up to this point? Do you have a lot of what you want, what you dreamed of? Are all your relationships thriving? Do you have a love partner, a companion, a best friend, unconditional love? Yes? Somewhat? Maybe? No? If you answer anything but yes to all those questions, then you must have a lot of what you don't want. The Law of Attraction is constantly working and being influenced 100 percent by your EMM beliefs if you're not paying attention. You don't deserve to experience a compromised life. Do you want better everything or more of what you already have? Do you want to stop all the drama and abuse? Do you want to stop stopping yourself from creating the life you desire and deserve? Then keep reading!

# chapter 5

## The Crazy Things Kids Believe

Tony called one afternoon and told me his wife bought him a gift certificate to have a psychic reading with me. She never had a reading with me but had been following me and listening to my interviews on podcasts and my Unity radio show. She thought I could be a great help for Tony.

"That's great, Tony. And you made a good choice by using the certificate. It says a lot about where you are right now in your life."

I told him about my arrangement with the Universe and being the Big Leap psychic, then continued. "So, no matter how you came to have an appointment with me—a gift, referral, seeing me somewhere, or even

Googling me—it means your soul is trying to tell you you're ready for a powerful transformation. I see the deep stuff that may be getting in the way of where you want to be in your life as well as the stuff that will get you there," I said preparing him.

"That's exactly what I'm hoping for," Tony said.

"Then be prepared because it will get heavy here. Are you ready for that, Tony?"

"I'm more than ready. You can tell me whatever I need to hear," he replied. "And don't hold anything back."

After giving him my typical instructions and process, I jumped right into it. I was getting bombarded with messages while instructing him. Some clients are so much more open than others because of their willingness to hear whatever is necessary for their evolution and dream achievement. The more open clients are, the more information and messages I can receive about and for them.

"I'm feeling you've been successful in the work you're doing and that you really enjoy that work. It's rewarding. Isn't that correct, Tony?"

"Yes, very!"

"Just yes or no."

"Sorry."

"That's okay. And you work with the public directly and provide a service that's nurturing and guiding in some way. Isn't that correct?"

"Yes."

"Very nurturing. Oh, wow! All of a sudden, I'm seeing a pair of wings on your back, so I feel your work is spiritual in some way. But you're not a minister of any kind, right?"

"That's correct. I'm not."

"It's very helpful and healing. You counsel people, but you're not a psychotherapist. I don't see any formal counseling degrees. There's part of me that wants to say you're a life coach, but I'm hearing that's not enough to describe what you do. I believe you're psychic, but you're not using that like I use it. I call myself a psychic. You don't. You call yourself a life coach or spiritual life coach. Is that it, Tony?" I asked to clarify what I was feeling.

"Yes, I'm a spiritual life coach. At least that's what I think I am," he said in amazement.

"No. You *are*," I assured him. "However, there's more. I personally don't know who you are but others do. Isn't that correct?"

"Yes. Not as known as you are."

"Maybe not right now you're not. Actually, you're playing much smaller than you are, Tony. You see yourself as a small fish in a large pond, don't you?"

"I'm trying to see myself bigger, but I can't seem to get beyond where I am now. Something seems to be blocking me."

"Hold on! Don't tell me too much. I can tell you right now that you're stopping yourself. Here is what I see from your soul about who you are. You're a messenger who came here to help heal the world. And you're very talented. You've written a book, haven't you?"

"Yes, but it didn't really go anywhere special."

"You mean it didn't become a *New York Times* best-seller, did it?"

"No, it didn't."

"But you still get mileage from it, don't you? I mean, you've gotten to do some events and talks, right?"

"Yes, I have, but nothing really as big as I would like to."

"Tony, do you know the phenomenon about a gold-fish?"

"No," he answered.

"You know those little goldfish you see in the little goldfish bowls that you can win at an amusement park when you throw a Ping-Pong ball into a bowl?"

"Yeah. What about them?" he replied.

"Do you know what happens to them when you pour them into a large pond or lake?"

"They get eaten," he laughed.

"No," I said laughing back. "They grow into those beautiful koi you see in ponds and lakes. You know, the big, beautiful ones that are gold, white, black, or mixed.

A goldfish as well as a turtle are the only two creatures that will grow to the size of the environment they're living in."

"Oh, I didn't know that," he said with surprise.

"I know. I'm psychic. A goldfish is a great metaphor for our capacity as humans and spiritual beings. We will grow to the size of our dreams no matter how big they are. However, there's one caveat that is different from a goldfish. A goldfish does it automatically based on its predisposed DNA. Humans need to believe they can grow to the size of their dreams."

"I thought I did believe that. I've done a lot of work on myself, Vincent, for the past twenty-five years," he responded with a hint of frustration in his voice.

"I know you have done a lot of work, and you have come a long way because of that work. But you're saying you want to go further. Well, then, just when you think you've done enough work, you haven't. There's always more to do."

I tried to be compassionate because the worst thing is to feel that all the work you've done to improve your life has been for no reason. It's *never* for no reason.

I continued, "This is the advanced class, Tony. I know what your dream is. You want to help and heal a lot of people. You want others to hear your message. Believe me, I know exactly what you're feeling, and that part isn't psychic. I can relate. You always thought you were special even as a little boy, didn't you?"

"Well, I suppose I did," he answered.

"Don't bullshit me. You can't lie to a psychic. Of course, you did. Otherwise, you wouldn't be drawn to the level of dream you want to achieve. Isn't that true?"

"Okay, yes."

"I know! I'm psychic, damn it! And there's nothing wrong with that. Jesus, Gandhi, Martin Luther King Jr., Nelson Mandela, and those other important figures who changed the world all had to feel special and inspired in some way to make such a difference. Otherwise, why would they think they had anything worthwhile to do or say? And why would they believe anyone would even listen? They all had to feel they had a special mission and something special to say. That's not to say they felt they were better than others, but they had to believe at least in this lifetime that they were special in some way. Let me really dive in your psyche and soul now. I'm already feeling why you have been stopping yourself, but I want to see the details."

I continued cautiously. "There are a lot of scars on your heart from past hurts. And you have a deep, dark place in your unconscious mind. A lot of abuse. Am I on track right now, Tony?" I asked guardedly. His voice changed to solemness.

"Yes."

"And the abuse seems to have come from different places. Isn't that also correct?"

"Yes."

"It started when you were quite young. Nine or ten years old. Isn't that right?"

"Yep." He was starting to get a more matter-of-fact attitude.

"I hear a lot of laughing, but *at* you in school. Did the kids pick on you in school, Tony?"

"They did."

"And it seemed to be all the time. In fact, you were physically abused there too. Isn't that correct?" My heart started to ache for him because it was becoming clearer to my senses that Tony was the subject of bullying in school.

"I was chased home from school almost every day. And if they caught me, they'd beat me up until I could get away," he said openly.

"Mom, Tony. I'm hearing Mom had something to do with all that bullying, didn't she?"

"Yep. Mom was disappointed I wasn't a girl when I was born. But I was very small and frail and very cute, cuter than my brother, so she used to dress me up very prissily, including when I started to go to school. She also always combed my hair perfectly. I was coiffed and dressed perfectly for school every day. Only the girls were dressed like that then. That's what began them picking on me," he explained.

"But that wasn't all, was it? I'm feeling something sexual happened in school also but nothing like rape and not from an adult. What the hell did they do to you? I can't get a clear enough picture. Do you feel comfortable enough to talk about it?"

"I can talk about it. In the school showers after gym class in junior high, most of the guys and jocks matured faster than me. First, they would make fun of my penis and testicles because they weren't as developed and big as theirs. And then one day one of the big football jocks held me while his buddy peed and then masturbated and ejaculated on me. Everyone left in the shower that day laughed at me, and I felt disgusted and humiliated."

"Dear God, of course, you would. And you never told anyone, did you?"

"Are you kidding? I didn't want anyone, including my parents or brother to find out."

Tony said defensively.

"But the abuse didn't end at school, did it? I'm feeling a lot more physical and emotional abuse at home as well. That's right too. Isn't it?"

"You're right about that too." Tony wasn't surprised anymore with what I was tapping into. He knew we were connected on a deeper level.

"Mom and Dad were also very abusive, weren't they? They beat you too!"

"Both Mom and Dad had some mental issues, and they took those issues out on my brother and I. Dad beat me more than Mom because he was her enforcer. He used his belt. Mom would hit us but with whatever she had in her hand, a wooden spoon, or metal one, a broom, or whatever."

"Lots of pain. Now Archangel Michael just told me that wasn't all the abuse," I interjected. "I'm getting something sexual again but more than what happened in the gym. You were sexually molested and more than once, weren't you, Tony?"

"Yes. By my babysitter until I was thirteen years old. It started at nine years old when we moved to our new home." He shared this intimate detail as if he had been talking about it his entire life.

"Shit, Tony! I'm surprised you didn't become a serial killer," I said jokingly but with some seriousness. "I'm so sorry you went through all of that. No kid should have to endure that."

He laughed with me. "It's okay. I did a lot of healing work," he said. "I've even forgiven everyone."

I was shocked that this man was talking with me on the phone like this, and I wasn't feeling any mental shit going on with him other than what I was going to soon tell him. It was obvious he did a good amount of healing work. However, Tony wanted to evolve to a higher consciousness level. He had bigger than the average dreams, which meant he needed to do bigger than the average inner work.

"I know you did. That's why you have come this far and achieved what you already have. But you want to go further and there's more work for you to do. Tony, you have taken care of, apparently, the issues that may have developed from all your abuse, but you have to remember that even though big Tony forgave everyone, understands nothing was your fault, and believes in himself, your inner child, little Tony doesn't share those beliefs. All injuries and hurts cause scars, and since little Tony was severely hurt, little Tony has scars. And you are an accumulation of your entire life, so little Tony with all his scars is still within your unconscious mind. And your unconscious mind is also where you're connected to the Law of Attraction. Little Tony has been blocking you from advancing to the level of your dreams without you knowing it."

I continued to explain so Tony understood completely how he was blocking himself. This is the part I always love with my clients because, as a psychic therapist, I can see and give my clients both their problems and solutions without waiting weeks, months, or years for them to come to their answers themselves as I had to as a traditional psychotherapist.

"There are actually two things going on," I intuitively shared. "First, you came into this world with a special mission but received anything but special treatment and nurturing. You didn't even receive the minimum required nurturing every child should get from their parents and environment. You received just the opposite. You were never noticed or recognized as the special kid you really were, and as you grew up, you developed an unconscious, intense need to prove yourself to the world and gain the acceptance and love you so longed for and were so deprived of. That need was your greatest coping mechanism, which saved your life and motivated you to do the work you're doing now. Bottom line is you're trying to prove you're special. Can you understand that part?" I asked.

"I guess I can. When you put it like that, I do understand what you're saying, but does that mean I'm making believe I want to be a spiritual counselor?" he asked with great concern.

"No, not at all! I believe *and* know you're doing what you're meant to be doing and doing it incredibly well but not for the right reason right now. That's one of the reasons you've only been able to get so far and no more." Before I could continue, Tony interrupted.

"What's the other reason? You said there were two reasons." He sounded a little frustrated.

"The other reason you haven't gone any farther is you don't believe what you think you believe about yourself. As humans, we have a great capacity to convince ourselves of anything even if it isn't true. And with that conviction, we can get places without the Law of Attraction working on our behalf. You've come this far in your career by sheer will and exhausting work. Isn't it true you've had to work your ass off to get even this far in your career?"

"Absolutely! And I feel that if I sit back at all I'll lose all that I've already gained," he expressed with concern.

"That's proof you've been working *against* the Law of Attraction. If you were feeding the Law of Attraction true beliefs about your dreams and worthiness to obtain them, it would have been easier for you to attain what you have now, including all that you want. Up until now, you've not been faking the work you're doing. You've been and are faking the belief that you're good enough and worthy enough to do it. Little Tony doesn't believe he is special anymore nor good enough to fulfill his soul's purpose. How could he? All the messages he received until his young adulthood were that he wasn't. You're not getting any further in your career as you desire because you don't believe you're good enough or deserving enough."

There was a long introspective pause from Tony. I let that sit with him until he was ready to continue.

"Okay. My work means more to me than anything else. What do I need to do now," he asked with a genuine desire to know.

"Well, first you have to change your belief from your work meaning more to you than anything else, to *you* meaning more to you than anything else. Your profound work and everything else you wish to manifest will come from there and only there," I corrected him.

I shared all the steps Tony needed to take during the rest of the session. He had several aha moments throughout the reading, and he expressed great gratitude for all I shared and for being forthcoming with him.

Over the past couple of years, Tony got in touch occasionally just to reinforce and validate all he is doing. He cares passionately about remaining on the right track. To date, Tony has significantly increased his business as well as his public visibility by interviewing on major television and radio shows nationally and internationally. He has even written another book that is being published.

Little Tony unknowingly still keeps trying to sabotage big Tony by telling big Tony that he isn't good enough, but big Tony is mindful and re-parents little Tony by constantly reminding and reinforcing that little Tony is a divine and magnificent child of God and special enough to create the life he wants and achieve all his dreams. Big Tony is growing to the size of his dream every day.

## Are You Lovable?

*Just when you think you've done enough work, you haven't.
There is always more to do.*

Were you nurtured to believe you're divine and magnificent and have unlimited abilities and could create anything you wanted? Were you inspired and motivated to
dream and dream big because there was no dream that
was too big for you to fulfill? Maybe instead you weren't
taught any of that. Maybe you experienced some of
what Tony did, maybe less or maybe more, or even what
Maria experienced. What beliefs do you think you could
have developed then?

The two most important things you learn from your
parents are (1) whether you're lovable and (2) how to love
yourself. Everything else you learn from your experiences out in the world. A child doesn't discover from
words what love means.

As I mentioned earlier, during the early developmental stages of the human mind, a child learns in concrete
terms, not abstracts. Behaviors, examples, interactions,
and primarily attention are the greatest concrete teaching tools adults need to rear a child. Words are mostly
ambiguous to the immature mind. "I love you" is a completely abstract phrase.

Of all the words in all human language, *love* is the most ambiguous. We use that word for so many different exclamations: "I love you very much." "I love this ice cream sundae more than anything." "I love being scared by horror movies." Then, the word can be used with conflicting reinforcement: "I'm doing this only because I love you," followed with a painful beating for something the child may have done wrong.

Therefore, a child learns he or she is lovable by the attention he or she receives. Hugging, praising, rewarding, even giving a child a desired cookie are all positive attention messages. The child will translate those attentions to being lovable. Then, reasonably, the reverse will produce the opposite belief of being unlovable.

It's as easy as this to understand. From birth to almost young adulthood, a youth translates all positive experiences into "I'm lovable" and all negative experiences into "I'm unlovable." As far-fetched as this may or may not sound to you, it's the truth and feeds us at our very core. This is another absolute concept you must accept.

Then, the actual treatment a child receives during youth, positive or negative, is the exact pattern by which the child treats themselves once an adult. Did your parents abuse you in some way, physically or emotionally? Do you abuse yourself today as an adult by being self-critical or possibly working yourself harder than you need like Tony did to counter your feelings of inadequacy? The latter is the result of the former no matter what excuses you can derive to argue the reason.

If you have no idea why you're stuck and can't continue to move forward or have distracting reasons in your life for not being able to reach your dreams, then you manifested those reasons because of how you translated the lack of proper attention you received to not being good enough, worthy, or lovable.

You truly have no idea how you interpreted your own experiences except by the outcome of your life. The extent of negative experiences you manifested into your reality is the extent of the negative Environment-Made Mind (EMM) beliefs you're containing. I said that before, but it bears repeating. On the helpful side, the extent of positive experiences you manifested into your reality is the extent of soulful beliefs that made their way through your EMM. I hope your ratio of positive to negative experiences is greatly skewed toward the positive. However, if it's not, fear not. That is the purpose of this book. You can remedy that skew and rapidly.

Most adults understand that sometimes children will get the wrong messages from the way they're treated, but a majority of adults, including some professional practitioners, believe children will grow out of everything, including their maladaptive beliefs. "They're just going through a phase" is the most common excuse experts use to calm parents. I'm here to set the record straight. Au contraire, *mes amis*. You grow out of nothing except your clothes. You grow into everything, or, shall I say, everything grows into you or into your EMM.

There's a misconception among many people about the idea of human aging. The idea of growing up is a fallacy based on most people's definition. To most, children grow up year by year to become adolescents, then adults, and finally seniors transitioning from one year to another. The teachings of doctors, researchers, psychiatrists, and psychologists instilled that perception. All of these professionals proposed the physical, mental, and moral developmental stages of humans.

I don't argue the stages at all. I'm reframing that idea so you understand why you can't leave your past behind. We don't grow up or transition from age to age. We grow out. We add another year to our previous ones. Technically, then, we are an accumulation of all our years over our entire lifetime. And, in truth, we are an accumulation of all our lifetimes, not just this one. To say we go through growth or developmental stages implies that one stage ends and another begins. That is untrue because, while we're in one developmental stage, we can easily digress into a previous one given the right circumstances and situations.

Why is this so important for me to point out? It's vital to understand that at this very moment, at whatever age you are, you have a collection of all your experiences, all your memories, all your thoughts, all your feelings, and all your beliefs stored within your mind. And as I said, you're an accumulation of all your lifetimes, so you can even have memories, thoughts, feelings, and beliefs from other lifetimes complicating the ones from your current life.

Many past clients and students have asked me if their current inability to create the lives they want stems from issues related to other lifetimes. My answer to them is always the same. Even if they do stem from another lifetime, everything is always correctable in your current lifetime.

Let me make a point clear to give you some comfort. There's absolutely nothing you created and manifested in your adult life that added any new negative self-beliefs into your EMM. You never have to heal new EMM beliefs—only the original ones. This is so important to understand that I want to state it again in no uncertain terms. As an adult, there's nothing you did to screw up your life. *Nothing.* No matter what crap you created for yourself and may still be creating, you never added to that original set of destructive beliefs in your EMM. You've only been compounding and manifesting from them throughout your entire life without knowing it.

I will explain why you're not adding more destructive beliefs to your storehouse as I continue to share new discoveries from my studies. However, for now, let me continue to illustrate how even our earliest beliefs formed in the EMM can manifest what we don't want into our current realities.

I knew nothing at thirteen about any metaphysical principles including the Law of Attraction and manifesting. The only things I knew that closely resembled manifesting were the ideas of consequences, or you reap what you sow from Catholic school lessons. If I did anything to piss off Mom, Dad, the kids in school, or God, I was going to earn a thrashing or a direct trip to hell. That's the extent of manifesting I knew.

The Law of Attraction, though, is neither about consequences or retaliation. It's about a power that can only say yes to everything you direct into it. If you say and believe, "I'm going to have a bad day today," the Law of Attraction part of the Universe says, "Yes. You will have a bad day today." It doesn't mean to go along with you when you send it bad vibrations. It has neither choice nor agenda for any of us and must perform its purpose—to create and bring into our reality that which we initiate.

Not wanting to beat this point to death, I want to help you clearly understand why the Law of Attraction works this way using Isaac Newton's first law of motion. Paraphrasing, his first law states that an object either remains at rest or continues to move at a constant velocity unless some other equal or greater force acts upon it. His theory can be applied to energy as well.

Therefore, the Law of Attraction is the object and energy that was put into forward working motion by God, the force. The Law of Attraction will continue to move in a forward direction unless something equal to or greater than God changes it. Since there's nothing equal to or greater than God that would change it, the Law of Attraction will always and forever work. Ah, but I psychically hear you shouting, "But you said God created us by becoming us, and, therefore, we have all God's abilities. Then can't we stop the Law of Attraction from working?"

That's a great question even if you weren't thinking it. You're right. God is everything and all energy and so are we. Being everything, God is the Law of Attraction and so are we. And in order for the Law of Attraction to stop working and existing, God and we would have to stop working and existing. However, also indicated by the laws of physics, energy can never be destroyed. Thus, energy can't cause its own demise, and thus the Law of Attraction can never be stopped. Therefore, you will always create by using it. How will you use it? Consciously or unconsciously? By your inner child's beliefs or by your adult beliefs? It's in your control.

What are some of the earliest conscious negative self-beliefs you may have formed from the messages you received from your world? Tony's Environment-Made Mind was on overload and worked overtime taking in all the negative beliefs he was feeding it from his torment and abuse experiences. Nothing was subtle in his life. The daily anguish was intolerable, and he developed multiple damaging and what seemed to be irreparable self-beliefs as a result. Our power to manifest is so great that even one negative EMM belief alone is capable of manifesting an undesirable experience. Can you imagine having a multitude of them, each one more negative than the other?

Have you halted or reached a plateau in your own journey? Do you feel stuck like Tony, not reaching the highest level of your dreams? Maybe you need to revisit the little you to see what messages or scars are still influencing your manifesting abilities.

chapter 6

# An Apple a Day Is Not Enough
## to Keep the Doctor Away

*M*any people call me to find out about their health. Some have legitimate, diagnosed health issues and want to find out when and if they will get better. Others have issues that aren't diagnosable because all the tests the doctors perform on them come back negative, yet they still feel ill or that something is wrong. Then there are those who are genetically predisposed to family illnesses and fear they're going to experience the same, so they turn to me to come up with some answers and solutions.

I'm no longer surprised at the number and types of illnesses people are experiencing today. The Centers for Disease Control and Prevention has lists of disorders, diseases, illnesses, and viruses too numerous to include here. Everyday a new illness or disorder appears worldwide. As a hospice clinical social worker, I saw all sorts of terminal illnesses. One of my patients even died from metastatic cancer that began under her pinky fingernail. Unbelievable!

I'm *not* a doctor nor am I a substitute for one; however, I am a medical intuitive and have saved several people's lives from sensing or seeing a serious illness or mass early enough to be fully treated and cured. I've also seen full-blown terminal stage-four cancer or severe diabetes but extended the lives of those clients by encouraging them to get to a doctor ASAP. They all went and are still here.

Though I can share hundreds of different stories of male and female client readings focused on health that I've collected over the past almost forty years of my psychic work, all of which are extremely interesting, I've randomly chosen one: Emily.

Emily made an appointment for a phone reading and wrote in the note section of my scheduling site that she searched for a psychic and found me on the internet and that something told her I was the one she needed to see.

"Good morning, Emily. How are you this morning," I began the call.

"I'm nervous," she replied.

"Nervous? Why?"

"I'm afraid of what you're going to tell me."

"Oh, don't be. I don't see anything bad unless you can do something to change it. If your soul wants out of here, and you can't do anything about that, I won't see that because what's the point? I don't want to make you depressed until you die! So, if you die tomorrow, don't come back to haunt me because I didn't tell you today," I jokingly said to break the ice and make her laugh. She did.

I went into my normal routine, then started her reading.

"I'm feeling you have a lot of questions for me today, but I would like to scan your soul and see what it is you need to hear consciously first. If I don't answer your questions during the reading, you can ask them at the end."

"Okay. Thanks."

"The first thing that is popping up for me that we need to focus on today is your health. I feel there are a lot of things going on in there and that you're not surprised to hear this. Isn't that correct, Emily?" I stopped to confirm.

"You're spot on," she replied. "That's what I'm afraid to hear about," she added.

I explained to her about me being a medical intuitive and not a doctor and the difference between both. "No matter what I tell you today about your health, Emily, you need to check everything out with your doctor if you haven't already. Do *not* take my word for medical advice or treatment. Do you understand that?" I asked for assurance.

"I understand. I just want to hear what you see," she replied.

"The first thing I want to start with is your blood. I'm feeling an imbalance in your blood. Your sugar level is off, isn't it?" When it comes to medical insights, I take a step at a time.

"It is."

"In fact, it's pretty high, isn't it?"

"Yes, it is," she affirmed.

"You have diabetes, don't you, Emily? And it's serious, isn't it?" I stated both questions plainly.

"Yes to both questions," she responded nervously.

"Don't worry. You're not going to die from that—yet. That's why you were inspired to make an appointment with me." I tried to lighten it up a bit to make her less nervous. She chuckled, and I continued. "And we're going to turn that around, aren't we, Emily?"

"I hope so," she said with a laugh.

"But you do need to seriously take care of it, which you're not committed to. I'm right, aren't I?" I asked pointedly.

"Yes, you are. I try. I need to take care of myself more. It's not easy because I also have—"

I cut her off. "Don't say anything else. Let me continue to see what else I get, and then I'll go into what you need to do to help heal everything or at least stop it all from getting worse." I wanted to already suggest I saw answers for her problems.

"Okay. Sorry."

"That's all right. I'm also sensing a lot of pain in your back as well as your joints, but they're coming from two different issues. The pain from your back is coming from disk problems in your lower back. Correct?"

"Yes."

"And the disk problems aren't from something chronic; that developed with age. It feels as if something caused them like an injury. Let me clear up the pictures I'm seeing before I ask you to confirm or deny what I'm saying. It wasn't at work. It wasn't at home. A car. It was in a car. You had a car accident," I finally said with confidence. "And it caused a lot of damage, didn't it?" I added.

"Yes, I did, a couple of years ago," she popped back with surprise at my process. "And you're right. It did cause a lot of damage."

"But it's been getting worse, not better?" I stated as a question though I knew the answer.

"Unfortunately, yes. I go for PT, the chiropractor, and acupuncture, but it's still getting worse. The disks are herniated and degenerating, and, because there are a few of them that were damaged in the car accident, they don't want to do surgery because two of my bones and disks are involved, and they don't want to fuse them altogether. I'm in so much pain," Emily added.

"I said you were in a lot of pain, but your joint pain is coming from something else—an inflammation and suppression of your immune system. Have you also been diagnosed with an autoimmune issue?" I asked curiously.

"I have rheumatoid arthritis as well," she said.

"Oh, my God, Emily! And you're still only in your fifties, right?" I asked in shock.

"I'm fifty-three," she answered with a tone of embarrassment.

"But I'm still feeling more than all those issues. What's going on with your eye now? One of them. The right one? There's something causing you to have vision problems in your right eye. What the hell is that now?" I asked with disbelief. I sometimes want to put myself at their level of disbelief with what is going on in their lives. Clients appreciate it when they get a sense that I understand what they're going through.

She snickered at me getting that too. "That's also right. I just found out last week I have this rare problem that I can't even pronounce the name of that is causing me to lose vision in my right eye. My eye doctor says I might eventually lose my vision in it completely. She just doesn't know when, and there's nothing anyone can do for it because it's so rare. What else could go wrong?" she said with defensive laughter.

"A *lot* more can go wrong!" I replied raising my voice. "Emily, that's all unbelievable! I can't believe you're going through all that. However, you *have* to stop all of that and start healing yourself," I stated firmly.

"What am I doing to cause all this?" she asked, not understanding.

"You're manifesting it all," I came right back. "Unconsciously, without knowing it, of course, but you're creating all of your illnesses and issues."

"I can maybe understand my diabetes because I haven't really been eating the way I should, but what about the accident? And my arthritis? How did I manifest all that? And now my eye disease?" she asked.

"You're talking with a psychic therapist and medium, so obviously you think outside the box. And you already know different spiritual and metaphysical principles, right?" I asked.

"That's right. I've done a lot of reading and attended a lot of classes," she confirmed my intuition.

"Then you know there's no such thing as a victim in this life, even when it comes to your health." I had to explain this very important understanding.

"This is an orderly world, Emily. Even the cells in our bodies act in an orderly manner. Victimization suggests something can happen spontaneously. Spontaneity and randomness mean the same. And you can't have randomness in an orderly universe. They're like oil and vinegar that don't mix. Do you understand at least that much?"

She hesitated, but then replied, "Yes, I do. That makes sense from what I already know."

I continued my explanation. "Here is more of why we aren't victims to even our health. We are spiritual beings having a physical experience. That means we are energies having a physical experience, and energy manipulates matter. That is a scientific understanding. That's also what God meant when Source created us and said we would have 'dominion' over everything physical on this planet. Our high vibrational energy surpasses all other energy and physical matter. Our bodies are physical, so our energy affects our bodies. And however we charge our energy, positively or negatively, our bodies will be affected by those charges. Does that also make sense, Emily?"

"Okay, it does. So, then what did I do to cause all my illnesses?" she asked.

"Don't think of it as what you did to cause your illnesses. That almost makes it sound like you purposely did something. You didn't know you were manifesting your illnesses and accident," I said trying to comfort her.

"Okay. Well, at least that makes me feel a little better."

"And think of this. If you manifested them, you can unmanifest them as well. We just have to figure out why you manifested them first." I went into the explanation of how we unconsciously and consciously manifest illnesses, which I will share in this chapter; then I continued with *why* she manifested them.

"Emily, you have three siblings, don't you?"

"Yes, I do."

"I'm feeling a lot of nurturing on your part even as a child. Am I correct?"

"You are."

"You had to nurture your brother and sisters, didn't you?"

"I did since I was real young. I was the oldest."

"Was there alcohol abuse in your family, one or both of your parents?" I asked to clarify.

"Yes, they were both alcoholics," she answered plainly.

"Yes, and as long as you took care of them, that's how you then believed you were a good girl and lovable. And you have been following that pattern to obtain love ever since. Haven't you been taking care of your family members again?"

"I took care of my brother while he had cancer. He was all alone and my sisters both live in other states," she explained.

"That was your choice, Emily. It didn't have to go that way because there are plenty of people and services out there willing to help in those situations. I know. I was a hospice social worker. You continued the role you took on when you were a little girl. But he's not the only one you took care of or have been taking care of now. Isn't that also true?" I asked again.

"I also took care of my father. He had cirrhosis of the liver until he died, and my mother wasn't capable of taking care of him."

"I'm not surprised," I replied. "But, again, you weren't the only one who was able to take care of him. You could have asked for help." Before Emily could respond, I added, "And I know you're going to say you tried, but your sisters and no one else could, right?" I took her silence as a yes.

"But you're not done," I continued. "Are you? Your mother is still alive, isn't she, and you're now her caregiver?" I asked in shock.

Hesitantly and demurely, Emily replied, "Yes, I am."

"Wow! Just wow is all I can say." I had made my point. "And you're becoming sicker every day." I said, "I know you have in your head you're the only one who can help your family, and it's wonderful you care enough to, but you're taking care of others at the expense of your own health. That's not just from your compassionate nature or boundless love of your family."

I continued to explain to Emily. "Understand where this all comes from. We all have the need to feel loved by learning we are lovable. If that need is not fulfilled during our childhoods, we strive to fulfill it for the rest of our adulthoods. The only caveat is that once we become adults, no parent, sibling, family member, or even friend can ever fulfill that need in us. As adults, only we can. Little Emily has been trying to get love from your brother, father, and now your mom all along. Your illnesses are proof of the true reason you have become everyone's caregiver. True unconditional love once received is empowering. Only Earthly, emotional need-based love is draining. And, as I will tell you about the four reasons we manifest illness later in this chapter, you're certainly unconsciously or consciously creating an excuse to be able to stop all your caregiving. However, you also don't want that excuse to take you out of here." I paused to let that sit with her.

"Can you understand that?" I asked compassionately.

"I do."

"Really?" I questioned again.

"Yes, really. So what do I do now? I don't want to die, and I don't want to be taking care of anyone anymore," she stated with exhaustion in her voice.

"Well, you already just started. Admitting that is the first and most important step. The process is easy from here on. It's the practice that's difficult because of how ingrained your habits are and also how ill you already are. But you still have time to turn that all around. Otherwise, you would have never been inspired to contact me. Remember, I'm the transformational psychic guy," I lightheartedly professed.

Emily laughed. "I'll try my best," she said.

"No. 'Do or do not. There is no try!' Remember what Yoda said," I came back at her.

During the remainder of time we had left in her session, I shared different steps and practices she could apply to help change her maladaptive beliefs developed in her youth that eventually led to her current illnesses. I also provided her with specific emotional steps to heal each individual issue. We ended Emily's reading with her feeling hopeful that her life was going to change. I expected the next year to be a more positive year for Emily.

## Are You Unconsciously Compromising Your Health?

Spirit is life. Mind is the builder. Physical is the result.
—Edgar Cayce

As you get older and your thinking and reasoning capacities mature, your ability to develop convincing and strong Adult-Made Mind (AMM) defense matures as well. Indirectly, the world supplies you with the elements you use to develop defenses. For example, you hear criticisms about the boss at work not being fair and that the boss doesn't appreciate the employees. You have your annual review with that boss, and you don't receive the compensation and promotion you were expecting. Your initial response might come from your EMM (Environment-Made Mind) by thinking, "I didn't do a good job. I'm not good enough." However, because your mind is quicker and more mature now, you develop a defense belief instead: "Damn. I didn't get my raise and promotion because the boss is an asshole."

AMM beliefs are remarkable in a way because in one aspect they help us to function in our daily living. We would be completely unproductive and dysfunctional living from our EMM beliefs only. Thinking, "I'm not good enough," "I'm not smart enough," "I don't deserve anything good," "I'm not attractive," "I'm not worth anything," or "I'm not lovable" throughout the day would paralyze us. The AMM beliefs that develop become our mechanisms for coping. People without strong AMM defenses experience significant emotional pathologies.

Depression and anxiety are two major disorders caused by strong EMM beliefs and weak AMM defenses. Strong AMM defenses help us get through life. Nonetheless, don't confuse surviving with living. AMM defenses cause us to do nothing more than survive in life or just exist. You can't manifest anything worthwhile from your AMM because that isn't where you manifest. And though you may be able to cope and exist because of your strong AMM defenses, you're most likely causing yourself irreparable strife, disappointment, and pain from what you're manifesting from your EMM. Remember, the stronger your AMM defenses, the less you're able to see the beliefs you're harboring in your inner child's mind or EMM, which is where you're truly manifesting from.

AMM defenses can become so controlling they can keep you from recognizing truths. Anxiety is one of the most prevalent hidden emotional disorders experienced by the majority of people in the world. Not only is it hidden from the public, it's also concealed from the people experiencing anxiety. In other words, people don't even know they're feeling full-blown anxiety until someone else points it out. How it reveals itself is through physical ailments like high blood pressure, skin disorders, food sensitivities, and a host of other psychosomatic conditions. Anxiety is also expressed in your dreams. Nightmares or intense and chaotic dreams reflect unresolved anxieties.

Also, a phenomenon that people have been experiencing worldwide—waking between 3:00 and 4:00 in the morning—has become completely accepted as part of their daily sleeping ritual although it's a major sign of anxiety. And the reason you're unaware of your anxiety is because your AMM is trying to protect you from your negative emotions.

As with Emily, the issue she is having with her eye could most definitely be coming from the anxiety she has been experiencing even though she's not feeling anxious. Her Adult-Made Mind (AMM) has shielded her from her anxiety, but it's there. From all the care-giving she has been doing, especially when she truly never wanted to, her AMM could be suppressing her anxiety, which is now bursting out in the form of her eye disorder.

The problem is the human brain doesn't take into consideration the damage it may be causing due to the defenses it has created. Our brain's highest and most important function is to keep us alive. It will protect us from biological as well as emotional attacks. However, as high functioning as it is, it never weighs the conse-quences. For example, let's say you just climbed Mt. Everest in your earnest desire to achieve new heights (my attempt at humor). After reaching the top, you find yourself gasping for air. In its immediate physical pro-tective response, your brain causes you to pass out, to lie your body down horizontally and unconsciously, since this is the easiest and fastest way for you to take in more breath and get more precious oxygen. That's why we pass out—to get more oxygen.

However, what the brain didn't take into consideration before making you pass out was that you're standing on a cliff, so you pass out to gain immediate oxygen for your body's survival, but as a result you fall off Mt. Everest to your death. I'm illustrating in this way because the first line of defense enacted by the brain isn't always beneficial to living a quality life or to living at all. The fight-or-flight syndrome occurs for the same survival reason. An instant secretion of adrenaline to either gain heroic strength or muster the speed and impulse to run away from danger can still result in death.

The same kind of reaction occurs within the brain to protect you from emotional threats. You suppress, repress, intellectualize, rationalize, or deny your anxiety until it eventually wreaks havoc on your body, and it will. Nonetheless, you're convinced you have no anxiety or any issue. This is only a tiny example of the results of these hidden emotions and beliefs. The most critical example is your health.

Your health is a direct result of all the negative emotions you have suppressed in your unconscious mind. Remember I said we are energies having a physical experience. Well, energy manipulates matter, and matter is everything physical. Your body is physical, so negative emotions create negative pockets of energy. Based on the laws of physics, energy can't be destroyed. Therefore, existing energy is transformed into a pocket of negative energy whenever you experience a negative thought or feeling.

Where do those indestructible pockets of negatively charged energy go? First, they become packed away in your EMM. Second, they feed into the universal energy, which affects all other life on Earth. That's how we as beings can affect and create the storms, earthquakes, tsunamis, tornadoes, fires, and all sorts of natural disasters on this planet. If we can cause all of that as a whole, can you imagine what havoc we can cause to our bodies individually? By not acknowledging those suppressed negative feelings, you literally can implode. This is the hardest concept for humans to accept—that we cause our own illnesses, diseases, and pains.

Feeling bad emotions doesn't cause bad health. In fact, you must feel to heal. Storing them away, ignoring them, and creating defense mechanisms to keep you from acknowledging them causes illnesses, accidents, and cancers. I spend most of my time in sessions bursting people's bubbles and breaking down their walls just to get them to see what they're really feeling and believing about themselves rather than the protective façades and masks they've created.

There are five reasons people experience illness or injury of any kind. Four of the reasons are unconscious that compromise their health, and one is conscious. That's right. Sometimes people will compromise their health consciously—with intention. I don't mean to say they would intentionally drink some poisonous liquid to purposely make themselves ill, although there are those with mental pathologies who would. I mean some people willfully won't take care of themselves or will feed into a minor illness to obtain a specific outcome they're desiring. I'll discuss that more as I present the four reasons of illness manifestation.

The first reason is the most common of the four, which I've already shared: **suppressed or repressed unresolved negative beliefs, feelings, behaviors, or thoughts**. Just to clarify, suppression is the process in which we consciously choose to push something out of our minds so we don't have to deal with it. In actuality, we're pushing it *deeper* in our minds and out of conscious awareness. You can't push anything *out* of your mind. Once thought or felt, it's in there forever. Repression is when the brain itself or AMM does that for us to protect us. Repression usually happens when we experience something very traumatic, which is why some people can't remember the experience.

Suppressing and repressing, then, will create pockets of negative energy that will become harbored in our minds but also possibly in a specific area of your body metaphorically connected to the negative belief or emotion. For example, maybe you've been diagnosed with rheumatoid arthritis like Emily, which causes a lot of pain and inflammation in your joints as well as else-where. This disorder is the direct result of suppressed anger.

What do we do when we get really angry? "Oh, I'm so angry!" We clench our fists and tighten up all our muscles, right? That puts stress on all our joints and ligaments. Hold that position for some time, and you will begin to feel pain. Well, suppressing anger for any length of time will do the same thing; it tightens you up emotionally. Thus, after a while that translates physically into some type of body pain. All arthritis, fibromyalgia, neuropathies, or any other physical pain issues all stem from the same suppressed anger. A person at peace has relaxed muscles and limited stress—and very little pain.

According to the World Health Organization, two of the top ten health disorders that kill people are heart disease, number one, and diabetes, number nine. Both are caused from self-love issues. Your heart is your fourth spiritual center. It's where we feel some of our most intense emotions—joy, bliss, happiness, heart-ache, grief, and, most importantly, love. Blood is the life force of the human body while love is the life force of the soul. Without either, we don't exist. If you experi-enced anything in your life to "clog" love from being felt in your heart and you have packed those clogs away, you can experience all sorts of issues in that area—diabetes, heart or lung disease, high blood pressure, and a host of others—as Emily has.

These are just some of the health issues you can experience from unresolved emotional and mental issues. The whole reason we gave ourselves seven major chakras, also labeled by Edgar Cayce as our seven spiritual centers, was to be able to discern the emotional, mental, or spiritual areas we need to work on and heal to live the lives we deserve.

For every illness and disorder, there's an emotional, mental, or spiritual deficit within your EMM and AMM. Two excellent resources to help you figure out what it is you need to work on emotionally and spiritually every time you experience any health issue, even if it's a toothache, are the Edgar Cayce material you can research at edgarcayce.org and the book *You Can Heal Your Life* by Louise Hay. I have a copy of that book sitting on my living room coffee table for anyone to pick up and read. It has an index in the back listing some of the most common ailments, the emotional aspect(s) you need to take care of, and an affirmation to help you with it.

The second reason you can become ill is **illness can give you a great excuse**. It can give you a good excuse to leave that damn job you hate because you don't have the confidence or self-belief to look for one you'd like better. It can give you an excuse to not work at all because you never found your passion or heart's desire because you were made to believe you weren't good enough or worthy enough to achieve it (remember Sean in an earlier chapter?).

Illness can give you an excuse to not have to help others anymore because you're tired of people asking you for help. It also gives you an excuse to get others to help you because you never believed they would want to get out of caring for you. And like Emily, it can give you a great excuse for not having to be a caregiver anymore or at all because the reason you became one to begin with was to gain love the only way you learned how.

According to the US government statistics, more than 10 million people are on Social Security Disability (SSD) and not having to work. And that only reflects the number of people that were approved to be on SSD. There are millions more in the United States alone suffering from some form of disability or physical ailment all for the same reasons I detailed in the previous paragraph. It's this second reason for becoming ill I said could be caused unconsciously or consciously. There are many unhappy people who tell themselves if they were ill they wouldn't have to work.

The third reason for illness is another biggie. You can actually see this reason posted all over all the different social media sites. You know those posts about the "horrible" illnesses, surgeries, accidents, or whatever terrible thing happened to them? Why do people do that? Why does anyone hang out their dirty laundry on those sites at all? To ask for prayer or consideration? It may seem that way, but that's not mostly true. There's only *one* reason most people do that. **For attention**. That's right, attention.

You might be asking, "So I became ill just so that I can receive attention, Vincent?"

Yes, reader, you may have. Think for a moment. As a child, when did you receive the most attention and possibly the most comfort? When you were ill. When I was sick, which was quite often in my youth, neither Mom nor Dad hit or yelled at me. It truly was the only time I can remember Mom would sit by my side and hold my hand or stroke my hair lovingly.

You think as an adult you don't need that same care and attention? Well, you're wrong. Besides, your inner child is in control of your unconscious beliefs, not your adult conscious mind. Your EMM beliefs influence your reactions and manifesting 24/7. If you don't believe me, when you're sick for whatever reason and your partner acts noncaring or inattentive, how much does that bother you? And don't lie now. You can't lie to a psychic!

I personally knew someone who was divorced and feared losing her children. As her children became older and more interested in their outside worlds, their mom became sicker and sicker and always required some care or attention from her children. When they were young adults, they began to believe Mom had become a hypo-chondriac to gain attention, and they became more and more wary of helping her, so they pulled away and gave her much less attention. That bothered their mom very much. There was a time, out of frustration and to guilt her kids into caring for her, she said to them, "You'll see! One day I'm going to be so ill you'll be sorry!" Well, that day came. Mom consciously and unconsciously mani-fested stage-four renal cancer that got her the attention she wanted but only for about two years. Mom died.

The fourth reason for becoming ill is a most diffi-cult one because it scares most people: it can be a way to leave here, check out, quit, give up. **Unconscious suicide** is quite prevalent across the world. People's souls are wanting out of here because life has become so stressful and filled with drama and trauma. Sometimes it's not your soul that wants to leave. It could be your conscious mind wanting to give up, but you would never commit conscious suicide, so your unconscious mind takes over.

Remember, I said earlier that 95 to 98 percent of your entire mind is in unconscious awareness. That holds a lot of power over you, which is why I've written this book—to gain conscious control over that which is unconscious. Unconscious suicide is more rampant than conscious suicide.

The number of people you hear dying from differ-ent ailments and disorders has increased over the past several decades and has become alarming. Aneurysms, heart attacks, accidents, strokes, not waking up from sleep, and the coronavirus are all ways souls are leaving here. Even those killed by mass or individual shootings, bombings, or war aren't all getting caught up in being in the wrong place at the wrong time. Some of their souls put them there intentionally to get out of here. I know that sounds outrageous, but remember we're not victims to anything that happens to us. We're either not listening to our inner guidance to keep us out of harm's way, or we're intentionally putting ourselves there. And, yes, children's souls leave, too, either for karmic reasons or other choices that are too difficult to accept. That's something to share in another book.

My dad is a perfect example of what the soul is capable of. In October 2009, at ninety-two years old, my dad had just received a clean bill of health from a full physical exam including lung X-rays and full body MRIs and was told he had the blood pressure of a teenager. At the same time, at eighty-six my mom gave up on life after a fall and the resulting hip fracture and was failing to thrive. We put her under hospice care, and on November twenty-third Mom died.

Dad, her partner for over sixty years, experienced a significant mental shift. We knew he would be leaving soon, too, because the two of them were inseparable, and my brother and I and our spouses were okay with that. We just didn't know how he was going to leave, considering he was so healthy.

Six weeks after Mom died, we had to hospitalize Dad because he had become catatonic. Though conscious, he couldn't respond to us. After hospitalizing him and requesting minimal testing, it turned out he had developed a lung tumor the size of an orange that was impinging on a major artery and sending cancer throughout his body. It caused metastatic bone cancer everywhere, and his catatonia was his brain protecting him from severe pain. They put him on morphine, and he became completely conscious again and pain-free.

We were about to bring him home and put him on hospice care, but that morning he started to have congestive heart failure. With no discomfort at all and having had a full breakfast and seeing my mom visit him, he died peacefully that evening on January 13 at 6:13 p.m. in room 413 of the hospital after being moved from ICU 13 on his half birthday. Dad was born June 13, 1920. That was a validation to all of us that his soul planned his entire leaving.

This fourth reason for illness tends to leave people with the grievous feeling that their loved one didn't have to die, and they're correct. The loss of a loved one is always painful no matter the cause or the reason. However, each person, each soul has the free will to choose his or her own journey and his or her own choices no matter how they affect the rest of us.

The fifth reason for illness is the most foolish one: **self-punishment**. That's right. There are people who believe they deserve to be ill and to suffer to make up for some grievous acts they did in their pasts. They just can't forgive themselves, so they punish themselves. We get that attitude and belief from the "an eye for an eye" philosophy or retribution principle. The retribution notion is that you must be punished for a wrongdoing. This idea created history's worldwide penal system.

The retribution concept has gone so far that there's an extreme Christian religious sect of monks that goes around whipping their bare backs all day because of their guilt over Jesus being crucified for their sins. An eye for an eye dates back to the beginning of society. If a tribal member of a group killed a tribal member of another group, whether by accident or on purpose, the other tribe had the right to take a member's life of the guilty tribe to make up for the death. At first, this was an understood practice. The different groups didn't like this arrangement after a while, which is what led to battles and wars between them.

Mercy and restitution allow for forgiveness of self and others. Restitution is knowing you made a lower choice, and you will do your best never to make that decision again. You don't have to contract some outlandish or painful disorder to punish yourself for your worst choices.

Discussing these five reasons for illness and injury is always difficult for me because people don't want to hear that they're the cause of their own suffering and possible terminal illness. Cancer-affected clients are some of the worst. "Am I going to die?" "Did I cause this?" "Will I be healed?" These are a few of the questions I get asked when people call me purposely to read into their future and tell them their prognosis.

My own best and dearest friend, who wanted to be involved in everything I was learning and experiencing when I first had my spiritual transformative event, contracted adult acute leukemia when he was only thirty-three years old. The first day after he was rushed to Mount Sinai Hospital in New York, I went to see him. Someone was there visiting him, and he looked as if he couldn't wait for his visitor to leave to ask me his most important question.

"Am I going to die?" he immediately asked with great fear in his voice and eyes.

"That's not the question you should be asking me. Your soul will decide that answer soon enough. You should be asking me what I need to do now." That was the only answer I could give him. He had work to do while still breathing.

As I said to Emily, if you're meant to die and can do nothing about it, I wouldn't see that. However, if you were going to die from getting into a car accident because you had too much to drink, I would see that. That you can alter. In hindsight, since I wasn't able to see or know the answer to my friend's question, that was the answer I gave him.

My heart aches for you if you come to me with any illness because, knowing it was self-created without your knowing, I have to tell you that. But I then get to give you the steps to take to possibly heal yourself. I say "possibly" because your healing requires a lot on your part—unwavering faith and belief in yourself, unblocking those AMM defense mechanisms, and releasing your EMM beliefs. You also need the unwavering faith that you can heal. Can you heal? Absolutely! I wouldn't be writing this book if I didn't believe that with my heart and soul. You can heal everything in your life that needs healing.

I know while you have been reading this chapter, you've been asking yourself what you did to cause any of the illnesses, disabilities, injuries, aches and pains, or other discomforts you're feeling today. Well, of course, you can call me for an appointment to find out or do some research in the recommended material. Whatever you choose to do, do something. Don't just accept what you're experiencing, wait for it to go away, or even just apply the doctor's orders. Remember, the diagnosis, whatever it is, is the result of a deeper emotional issue and not an issue unto itself. And you *can* heal it. You're totally worth the effort!

chapter 7

No Pain, No Gain

As a race, we humans come up with some really dumbass philosophies and notions. One example of a delusional idea dates all the way back to ancient Greece quoted by historian and general Thucydides, who claimed basically that "might makes right." In other words, the powerful have the right to control the weak. This gave permission for the mighty Greek army to overtake and pillage weaker nations of which there were many.

These kinds of philosophies arise out of the Adult-Made Mind (AMM) as defenses to condone or excuse beliefs, behaviors, and actions. Though many philosophies help to guide our choices in a more positive direction, others hinder and defeat our abilities to man-ifest what we desire.

Some ideas and constructs that truly get in the way and stop us from our rightful abundance in life revolve around money. A few of the many bad ideas and notions that have sprung up over the centuries are "the almighty dollar," "the Midas touch," "live from hand to mouth," "keep our heads above water," "live within your means," "money doesn't grow on trees," "money isn't easy to come by," "money is the root of all evil," "not made of money," and one of the most commons ones is "you have to work hard for your money."

These ridiculous mottos have been taught to us by our parents, family members, friends, educators, bosses, and others and have caused poverty and a host of other financial issues among us all worldwide.

Since currency was created, some type of class, lesson, or lecture about finances and money has been passed down from generation to generation. Economics is a major subject and even a career. Money is a major part of every society, and our individual beliefs about it determine our own financial status throughout our lives until we die and even after. From the first coin or dollar bill you receive as a child as a gift or allowance, you begin to develop your beliefs about money. And those beliefs expand and mature as you grow, but your Environment-

Made Mind (EMM) never lets go of your original ones. And remember, whatever is in your unconscious mind creates your reality.

I had an appointment with Tom and his wife, Frances. Sometimes couples call together to try to split the time booked between them, but I don't work that way. It's not appropriate. I work with couples as one entity with the same questions, though information and messages will still come up for each of them individually. In this case, Tom and Frances shared the same issue.

"Hi, Vincent. This is Tom. I'm your two o'clock appointment. My wife, Frances, is on the phone too," Tom said.

"Hey, Tom and Frances. It's nice to be talking with you both. I'm glad you made the appointment together because what I will be sharing with you today, I need you both to hear," I responded. Clairvoyantly, messages were pouring into my mind already as I started talking with them. I gave them my introductory spiel and went right into the reading.

"I'm not sure yet why you both decided to make the appointment together, but I can tell you right now you both needed to. You both seem to be sharing a similar problem, and it's not about your relationship. That's going great, right?"

They both chimed in, "Yes, it is."

"It's been a long relationship too. Hasn't it been?"

"We've been together for forty-eight years and married for forty-four years," Tom announced proudly.

"Good for you two! I can feel you've both done some wonderful work together. You do a lot of things together, don't you?" I asked knowing the answer already.

"We basically do everything together," Frances answered. "Except Tom has his own work and I have mine. I sometimes go out to lunch with my daughter and friends, but that's about it," Frances added.

"You even attend some spiritual center together I'm being told by Archangel Michael. Isn't that also correct?"

"We do," they both answered.

"You also share some of the same problems, don't you?" I asked.

"Not all our problems are the same," Frances defended. "We do have some different ones, but, yes, some important ones are the same," she admitted.

"I know. The problem with couples sharing the same issues is that the issue becomes more difficult to reverse though not impossible," I explained. "What I'm seeing is going to require the two of you helping each other a lot, even more than you already have."

"Can you see what trouble we are having?" Tom asked.

"M-o-n-e-y!" I spelled with serious intention. "Money. You have issues regarding money. Isn't that why you booked this reading?"

"Y-e-s!" they replied mirroring each other. "We do!" Tom added, "I have my own business, and Frances has a great job, but we can never get ahead of the bills. I don't know how to make the businesses better. Nothing seems to be working."

"I know. That's why I'm a damn good psychic." Many times I add humor to lighten the reading, especially when I need to get really deep. "You both know like attracts like, right?"

"We do."

"Well, you both come from very similar financial backgrounds though with different stories. Frances, I'm not seeing your dad having been around, and when he was it was briefly. Your parents were divorced, isn't that correct, Frances?" I asked for validation.

"That's correct. We only saw Dad when we went to see him."

"And when you say 'we,' you mean with your brother and sister, correct?"

"That's right."

"So, Mom was a single parent with three children. She went to work after the divorce but didn't make a lot, did she?"

"No, she didn't. That's right."

"You needed financial help a lot of the times, didn't you?"

"We did."

"And it wasn't easy for Mom to ask for help either? Was it? Everyone around you had more money—family, friends. Right?" This was going fast by now.

"Yes."

"You sometimes got hand-me-downs from the relatives, and you were embarrassed," I added. "You, your mom, brother, and sister all developed a poor-man's attitude. And besides that, since children blame themselves for everything, you took on the beliefs that you don't deserve money and aren't worthy of a comfortable life. Money was taken away from you when your parents divorced and your father left."

"And he made a shit load of money too," Frances quickly interjected. "And you're spot on about everything," she added.

"Your dad did not support you all very well, did he?" I asked.

"No, he didn't. He hardly had to give any money to Mom for alimony or child support."

"I know. And you grew up with the beliefs that you were unworthy and not as good as the rest of the family. That money was only for the wealthy." I left Frances with those thoughts.

"And now for you, Tom. I'm seeing the lack of money in your past too. Mom didn't work when you were very young and then had to later on when you were older. Isn't that correct?"

"That's right."

"Dad didn't make a lot of money though. He was a blue-collar worker, wasn't he?" I asked with the feeling Tom's deceased father had just joined us. "Tom, your father is deceased, right?"

"He is," he said with curiosity.

"He's here with us right now. He told me he was a blue-collar worker in different factories and then he cleaned. He just showed me. Mopping floors? That's all I can make of what he is showing me. Isn't that very true, Tom?"

"Yes, it is. I was told his job when he married Mom was in a sewing factory. That's where he met her. Then he got a job bottling 7-Up soda. He lost his job there after he had an accident and fell off a ladder. After that he because a janitor for a high school. That was all he could get. That's while I was in high school. He couldn't get a job after he lost his with 7-Up because both my parents weren't registered as Republicans in the town we moved to on Long Island. They were actually told that if they didn't become Republicans, Dad wouldn't work on Long Island."

Tom shared his father's story to clarify what I was sensing and seeing. "Dad is saying he never had a good job because he wasn't smart enough," I went on.

"Dad had to leave school after the sixth grade to work and help his family. He had three brothers and one sister. So he never completed his education."

"Dad said he always felt blessed having such smart children. He didn't think he deserved you and your brother. You have a brother, right? And Dad told you that, didn't he?" I asked.

"I do have one brother, and Dad did tell us that one time. I just don't remember when he told us that."

"He said when the two of you were already men."

"Oh, yeah. I don't know why he told us though."

"Dad is telling me he wishes he had given you more. He just said Mom used to hit you so much because Dad didn't make enough money. Okay, you're going to have to explain that one, Tom," I stated, being a little confused with what I saw and heard from Tom's dad.

"They couldn't afford to get me and my brother a lot of different or good clothes. We only had cheap but good-looking, Sunday go-to-church clothes and then cheap but good-looking school clothes. And the clothes we *did* have had to last a long time. My brother and I were pretty physical, and every time we fell and got our clothes dirty, Mom would hit us. 'How many times have I told you not to get your clothes dirty?' Mom would yell at us while hitting," Tom explained.

"Well, Dad is really sorry for that. And also for hitting you when Mom told him to. Is that also true?"

"Unfortunately, yes," Tom answered.

I went on. "Dad wants me to explain this to you now. So you grew up with the ideas that money was hard to come by, you had to work really hard for it, and you had to be deserving in some way to get it. That's what little Tom believes," I informed him. I continued to explain.

"You see, both of you have had negative feelings about money all your lives because of your pasts."

Tom jumped in, "I always hated money actually because of how I see it changes people."

"That only added to all your other negative beliefs, and because of all your beliefs about money, you've actually been stopping yourself from making it or at least making a lot of it."

Frances attempted to correct me. "But we believe now it's okay to make money, especially since we had two kids, who are grown now, but we haven't been able to make more than just meeting the bills and sometimes less than that."

"That's right," Tom joined in. "Even if I start making more, something always happens for us to have to spend it."

"I get it," I validated. "However, your old beliefs are still in there, deep within your minds, and those are the beliefs that are influencing your money manifesting. Getting rid of old beliefs isn't easy, and the older you are, the more ingrained they are. Let me ask you this and be honest. You can't lie to a psychic. Do you both believe in your hearts that you deserve to be millionaires?"

"Well," they spoke in unison. "Well, I guess so. Yeah. Though we can't see how that will happen," Tom added.

"Then there you go. And you never will. You hesitated when you answered, which means you really don't believe you deserve to have abundance, and you can't imagine how you can become millionaires, so how on Earth can the Universe manifest it for you? Manifesting doesn't come from knowing *how* you can create something you desire. Manifesting is believing you can. You want to grow more financially secure? You need to do more inner work and get those beliefs about money changed."

I continued with further explanation. "Money is a blessing that came from a divine inspiration. And there's enough to go around, though there's a delusion out in the world that there's lack. *And* you can manifest it without busting your asses! There isn't enough time to tell you all the stories about people who went from having zero dollars in their bank accounts one day to money coming in unexpectedly from unexpected sources the next day. You both deserve not to have to struggle financially. You both deserve to be prosperous. I want you both to do this homework. Each of you on your own write in a journal one paragraph stating your greatest financial dream. Make it as big as you desire and believe you can have. Then compare your dreams. See how close they are. Also, see what you can add to yours. The idea is to come up with the best paragraph of a financial dream you both can focus on. Read it every day as often as you can. Feel the dream in your hearts when you read it. Read it out loud to each other or on your own. Then watch. Watch for the changes that begin to occur. It won't take long for you to begin to see growth in your financial situation. Keep reading your dream and make it even bigger if you can."

"Your lives are about ready to transform as I told you at the beginning of this reading, so be prepared and enjoy the transformations."

I finished up the reading. They both agreed that they needed to make mental changes, and they were anxious to do the work together and quickly. Six months later they booked another appointment, mostly to share how much they had been thriving financially. Besides doing the homework I gave, they both took a prosperity class from their spiritual center and loved it. Tom's business exploded with clientele after a surprise interview on a famous radio show and providing classes he was inspired to do, and Frances got an unexpected huge promotion at her job with a substantial salary increase. All within six months.

Does this sound too unreal to you? It happens all the time. Look at your own financial circumstances and examine your inner beliefs about money. Are they similar to Frances's and Tom's? Maybe worse? Maybe not as bad? It doesn't matter if you believe the same or not. If you don't believe you're deserving of financial abundance and that the Universe can provide for your needs plus a hell of a lot more, then you can expect to struggle until you can believe.

## Test the Philosophy of Prosperity

"Behold the fowls of the air: for they sow not, neither do they reap, nor gather into barns; yet your heavenly Father feedeth them. Are ye not much better than they?"
(Matthew 6:26 [KJV])

"Consider the lilies how they grow: they toil not, they spin not; and yet I say unto you, that Solomon in all his glory was not arrayed like one of these."
(Luke 12:27 [KJV])

Both these parables spoke of worth and abundance and said that if God provided for the creatures of the earth, what more would God provide us. You might not believe in any formal religion that teaches these concepts, but all you have to do is look at the evidence in the world. People *can* and *have* become instantly wealthy or financially secure overnight all from a change in their beliefs.

I challenge you, the reader, to test this philosophy of prosperity. Use my Three R System to start. First, go deep within and **review** your own constructs about money. What do you harbor within your Environment-Made Mind? What defense beliefs might your Adult-Made Mind have developed? If they're negative at all, the next thing to do is **replace** them with positive beliefs—money is easy to come by, everyone deserves to have enough money to live the lives they desire, you don't have to work so hard to have money, and money is a blessing. Say to yourself, "I deserve abundance!" Even if you have to fake it at first, do whatever you need to do to replace those negative beliefs and then **reinforce** the positive ones. Remind yourself daily of your new positive beliefs. Say them out loud as I told Tom and Frances to do and say them with feeling.

Commit to yourself to at least take on this challenge and then watch for the changes. Don't you deserve to live prosperously? Do you really believe that? Do you want to believe that? Then you can.

chapter 8

The Key

*L*et's summarize what I've shared so far. The majority of us are living by the control of the subconscious, the Environment-Made Mind or EMM, the Adult-Made Mind I call the AMM, and the conscious mind with an occasional influence from the soul's mind. And because of our powers to convince ourselves of anything, we believe everything in the AMM is real and the truth.

All the learning, applying, and trying you're doing to create better lives you're doing from your AMM, and you just can't process from there. That mind harbors your defenses and false beliefs. You take in information by way of various conscious levels, but to assimilate and believe in the information, you need to process it within your superconscious, using your soul's intuition as a filter. Recall that your superconscious mind resides all the way beneath your subconscious, AMM, and EMM. Therefore, even if the new information you take in is accurate and meant to be beneficial in some way, you're only processing it in your AMM and EMM and not in your deepest mind with the help of your soul.

Thus, the results from the application of the information are weak, not sustaining, and eventually break down over time. Combine this with the Law of Attraction process, and you become disappointed and disillusioned because those things you desire to manifest in your life are left unfulfilled.

Sometimes, you can even be conscious that you don't believe what you hope to believe. We've created comfortable-sounding metaphors to express this such as these: "I understand it intellectually but not emotionally," "I know it in my head but not in my heart," "It may be eight inches between my head and my heart, but it seems like a mile," "My head is telling me one thing, but my heart is telling me something else." These are all acknowledgments that you think you believe something but really don't.

Nonetheless, the power of the AMM can be so strong. With many people it can repress true maladaptive beliefs so deeply in the psyche, people can be walking around thinking they believe one way and completely act opposite to their beliefs, and nothing can convince them they're doing that. These blind people living in a world of denial can be clearly obvious to the rest of the world. We've seen people who are perfect examples of this truth over the past few years worldwide. A lot of hypocrisy has been going on.

We've even created jargon that distinguishes these people: "He talks out of the side of his mouth," or "She's two-faced," are common expressions. And as I said previously, it's why some people can believe they're truly good people even while they laugh at, judge, and are prejudiced toward others. There are even spiritual and metaphysical practitioners who are convinced they have pure and loving beliefs when their actions prove otherwise.

In any case, you're not applying the principles with the correct process. Consequently, no matter how hard and how many times you try something that you've seen work for so many other people, you end up saying, "It's not working." No matter how many procedures and formulas shared by highly successful people you attempt, you end up saying, "It's not working." No matter how much you pray and have faith, you end up saying, "It's not working." Even if you've taken *A Course in Miracles,* read *The Secret,* read Deepak Chopra, Wayne Dyer, Abraham (Esther) Hicks, Marianne Williamson, or any other luminary's book, in frustration you end up screaming, "Damn it, God, it's not working!" It's all because you don't really believe what you need to believe because what you need to believe resides deep within your superconscious and soul mind and not in your subconscious, AMM, or EMM.

The heat that turns the ingredients into a cake, the final process you need, the something you aren't doing that reconnects you to your magnificence, God, all the wisdom, all the knowledge, all your inner true guidance, and all your divinely endowed gifts is totally and unconditionally believing in and loving yourself. That's it. That's the key to making everything you attempt work. That's the key that even gets you to stop stopping yourself. It's the *only* key.

Like I said earlier, it's so simple and so trite that if I mentioned it any sooner, your own AMM would have said, "Oh, I know that already. I believe in myself," and you would have closed the book and stopped reading. And that's because you may have convinced yourself that you *do* believe in yourself. Chances are if you're reading this book, you don't believe in yourself, at least not as you should—unconditionally.

Let me show you right now whether you believe in yourself or not and to what degree. Let's use your life as it is currently as a barometer. The extent that your life isn't the way you would like it to be is the extent you don't believe in yourself. And because of the Law of Attraction, the reverse will follow: the extent that you don't believe in yourself is the extent that your life won't be the way you desire it to be.

**Barometer of Lack of Self-Belief.**

**Barometer of Self-Belief.**

On the flip side, if this is true, which it is, then the opposite is just as true. The extent that you believe in yourself is the extent that your life will be the way you desire it to be. You won't be able to help it. You'll manifest all you dream.

## Let's Get Real

*If you believe, you will receive whatever you ask for in prayer.*
(Matthew 21:22 [NIV])

There's a greater problem, though, than not believing in yourself. I'm sure you heard sometime in your youth or at least your early adulthood, whether from your parents or teachers in school, that you should believe in yourself. It's a common understanding of most affirmations. Since the dawn of modern psychology and then the New Age movement, spiritual and self-help books and courses all work at building self-esteem and belief. But these often lead to a shallow understanding, a false belief as opposed to a true and profound experience of unconditional self-love. As a result, your AMM kicks in overtime and either nothing or limited actions you attempt will work.

Your AMM works in two ways. First, it obstructs and blocks any messages attempting to come from deep within your psyche because it doesn't trust them. So if true self-belief is attempting to rise from your inner-core beliefs and soul's mind, your AMM blocks it. Second, it deceives and tricks you by creating a false sense of confidence your intellect knows you need. Remember, I said the brain and mind must protect you at any cost, so it will create a false sense of confidence that not only deceives you but also fools everyone else as well.

Research has shown that many suicides are successful because the distressed person fooled everyone, including himself or herself. It's not always the obvious severely depressed person who attempts or succeeds at suicide. Unconscious depression leads to suicide. It's not always planned as cleanly as you sometimes hear, and family, friends, and peers can be completely taken off guard and shocked by the suicide. The first response you hear from some loved ones of suicidal people is, "She/he seemed so confident."

Research also shows that most people think they have strong self-belief. And if it weren't for the spiritual laws of attraction, abundance, and manifesting, there would be nothing to prove otherwise. Whether you're aware or unaware of the principles that govern this Universe, you're all coming to the same conclusions about your lives. If you're not experiencing abundance by having a rewarding vocation, physical and mental wellness, financial security, loving relationships, and fulfilling dreams as you see others achieving and enjoying, there are only a few conclusions you can come to: You're just not as fortunate as others because of something you've done or something someone else has done. You weren't meant to experience the good life this time around. You don't deserve to experience abundance or the good life.

You're fulfilling some karmic debt. Or not everyone can fulfill their dreams. And if you're truly altruistic or believe you're more spiritually evolved than most, you may even believe the only way to experience your greatest essence and divine spirit is to not desire anything more than the Universe gives you.

Even Buddha professes that if you desire more than you already have, that leads to evil: "Desire is the root cause of all evil." I believe that saying actually is the most damaging belief because (1) since that belief sounds so good, it distracts you more from your true EMM beliefs that are packed away in you and feeding your AMM defenses, and (2) it actually does the reverse and keeps you from evolving because you stop striving for more goodness in your current life. You can't experience all of who you are if you give up the desire to experience more of who you are.

Jesus said, "Ask, and it shall be given you; seek, and ye shall find; knock, and it shall be opened unto you: For everyone that asketh, receiveth; and he that seeketh, findeth; and to him that knocketh, it shall be opened." (Matthew 7:7–8 [KJV])

Jesus was talking about a proactive, desirous life here, not just about how to accept what happens along the way, just going with the flow, or surrendering your wants. Nor did he say, "You may ask but only once." In fact, Jesus is so adamant about seeking what you desire, he repeats what he says here twice, using more active verbs the second time. Don't just ask, asketh. What beliefs do you have right now about your life? Why do you believe you don't have all you want? When you were reading about Angie, Sean, Maria, Ellen, and Tony and Frances, what of your own beliefs you were reflecting on?

The bottom line is you're unconsciously developing any or all those beliefs without realizing you only lack one: self-belief. Simply, you have lack in your life because you lack self-belief. Now understand that true unconditional self-belief doesn't wane. False self-belief or snippets of your soul's true self-belief making their way to your conscious mind do vanish, especially when you've raised the bar and the stakes are high.

Right now, you may be thinking, "Come on, Vincent. So every time I have a little doubt in myself, I don't really believe in or love myself?" Doubt alone is like a little gray cloud that comes along and covers the sun. Even though you can't see the sun in that moment, you know it's still there and will be shining through again shortly. When your self-belief and self-love are true, you're capable of acknowledging the doubt, recognizing that it's temporary, and helping move it along with some positive affirmations or behaviors. When the clouds, though, keep coming and going, chances are you're living from your false self-belief that wavers in strength. However, if it's always cloudy outside and you can't ever see the sun, you have no self-belief or self-love. The tiniest amount of true self-belief can move along even the largest bank of dark clouds.

Maybe you're thinking instead, "You're not talking about me. I know I believe in myself. You're talking about someone else." That's the denial defense. Then, again, you may be thinking, "I've been doing a lot of work on myself and I'm getting better." That's intellectualization. You may find yourself saying, "I've had a rough life. It's hard for me to believe in myself," or "Give me a break. Everyone has trouble believing in themselves." Those are rationalizations. The only thought you should be thinking right now is, "It may be possible that I don't believe in myself. I need to examine that."

Your soul's mind is confident and willing to embrace and examine any possibility, openly and without fear. Your soul isn't afraid to acknowledge any of your weaknesses. To find out what you believe, you need to be brave and let go of what you think you believe.

In 1992, at thirty-seven years old, I made up for sleeping in the university parking lot instead of attending my classes by beginning a full-time college expedition carrying a full load starting at Thomas Edison College, Middlesex College, and Rutgers University in New Jersey and finishing the journey with highest honors at the University of North Carolina at Chapel Hill (UNC-CH) with a bachelor of arts degree in psychology and a master's degree in clinical social work. While at UNC-CH, I had the opportunity to study with many accomplished and published psychology professors and scholars. It was at UNC-CH where my own intrinsic understanding about the human mind began to unveil itself. My focus and exploration were on the human "self" in personal psychology.

During my studies, one research article I found in a psychology journal contained these reasonable truths that were accepted by the psychological and psychiatric communities:

- Most humans are self-enhancing and exaggerate their traits and abilities; in fact, the higher their confidence and self-esteem levels, the more they're self-enhancing.

- The majority of humans compartmentalize their external lives as a means of coping, and the more compartments people have, the happier and more successful they feel.

- Since the majority of people self-enhance, it is reasonable to conclude that the majority of humans are at least slightly narcissistic.

Many other social psychologists conducted similar research only to arrive at similar theories. The statistics are so high for these conclusions that if there are five of you in your family reading this book right now, at least 3.5 of you are narcissistic and believe you're better than everyone else in your family. My curiosity revolved around the question, "Why?" To me, why people self-enhance was even more important to understand than the fact that they do.

These and other studies like these led psychologists, spiritual teachers, and authors alike to conclude that our egos get in the way of our genuineness, growth, and true evolvement. In my work as a psychic medium and spiritual counselor, I perceived and theorized just the opposite—the majority of individuals actually have low or no self-esteem. Having enhanced egos isn't their problem. Having little or no ego is. They're self-critical and self-denigrating. Self-enhancement did not seem to be the general population's real problem. I went back to revisit the studies and delve deeper.

I reviewed these studies along with the raw data on the self and self-esteem. Most were conducted at major universities with the age of the college students ranging between eighteen to thirty-five years old, but today the range would be greater with a greater number of older people attending. Because of the age range, the college attendee group is scientifically considered a normal sampling of the general adult population.

In some studies, random participants were asked questions about their general demographics, background, and experiences growing up. Then they were asked to list and rate the levels of their skills, talents, and intellectual abilities. Finally, the researcher reviewed the participants' education history and college records. If you just compare only the self-reporting answers with the actual history and evidence, the results do seem staggering on the surface. Based on researchers' findings, the numbers were as follows:

- 70 percent of the hundreds of participants surveyed did, in fact, report and rate their abilities and attributes higher than their actual history and evidence supported. They also reported having high self-esteem.
- 20 percent downgraded themselves worse than their true abilities.
- Only 10 percent listed and rated their abilities accurately.

The numbers were too significant and consistent to deny that at least the majority of the participants in these studies self-enhanced and claimed to have high self-esteem. Nevertheless, my intuition and persistence directed me to find out why 70 percent of respondents enhanced their actual abilities and reported they highly believed in themselves.

In reviewing their backgrounds and experiences during their youth, the participants reported of the 70 percent who self-enhanced and reported having high self-esteem, 100 percent of them reported coming from a dysfunctional family and experiencing some type of difficult past. Their descriptions of the family background included parents who were emotionally and physically abusive, substance abusers, divorced, single, financially stressed, impoverished, imprisoned, mentally challenged or ill, chronically ill, who died when the children were young, or who had other various pathologies. Everyone in that self-enhancing group had some type of negative story about his or her past.

Paradoxically, the 10 percent that reported their talents and abilities accurately stated that they grew up in stable, happy environments with functional, supportive, nurturing, and loving parents and family members. Those were huge, important polar dichotomies that needed to be better understood.

The psychologists and researchers interested in human self-imaging and assessment chose not to pay attention to all the factors and variables. The evidence was so compelling that it was more reasonable and responsible for the "experts" to conclude with significant support that all people who exaggerate their abilities and skill levels do so as a means of coping because they all come from dysfunctional backgrounds. Rather, they grossly concluded that the majority of people with high self-esteem exaggerate their attributes and are narcissistic to some degree.

The *actual* theory the experts were attempting to propose was the reason most people can't succeed at their goals and dreams: they did not have realistic views of themselves. Now, this is a completely different theory that I can agree with from all the work I presented in this book that has nothing to do with an "enhanced" sense of self. Ironically, this book and the discoveries I made were inspired from a similar idea but for quite different reasons. I took this past research further with my own unpublished research.

Right after discovering all the variables from these studies, I decided to replicate one of these research studies. I was still at UNC and had enough students to recruit new participants. I used the same questions and procedures with 100 random participants, and my study yielded similar results. About 70 percent self-enhanced, 20 percent self-denigrated, and 10 percent were accurate. Similarly, the 70 percent and 20 percent all reported having negative pasts. However, I did one thing differently in my study from all the other researchers.

I returned to the 70 percent of participants who enhanced their traits. First, I asked if they consciously chose to exaggerate themselves. Of the 70 percent who exaggerated their abilities, ninety claimed they didn't know they exaggerated. The other 2 percent refused to answer. Of that 2 percent, I took into consideration that there might have been a few who didn't wish to admit they knew they were exaggerating. Nevertheless, I had enough evidence to support that the majority of people who self-enhance don't even know they're doing so.

In addition, after further questioning of the group of participants at the end of the study, I discovered they also were unaware of any negative self-feelings or beliefs they had because of their pasts. They didn't know they were exaggerating, and they didn't know if they had any maladaptive beliefs about themselves. The workings of the Freudian-defined defense mechanisms, suppression and repression, were profound with these participants.

All the research subjects who self-enhanced in all these studies created new beliefs for themselves in their AMMs. Their EMM beliefs were painful, and their AMMs protected them by creating the false beliefs that they were better than what they really were, and they believed in themselves more than they really did. That's why their talents, abilities, and the outcomes of their lives didn't match up. Not only did they overrate their skills, but they also manifested lack in their lives due to their true EMM beliefs. This research became the foundation for my beliefs and theories.

By the time I obtained my degrees, I knew enough about narcissism to understand that it isn't just a personality disorder. A narcissist's grandiose self-beliefs are defenses created by his or her mind to compensate for unconsciously having extremely low and unhealthy self-esteem. In addition, the lower the level of self-esteem, the higher the level of narcissism a person can experience. Narcissism, then, is a result and not a trait. Narcissists don't consciously realize they don't really believe the grandiose things they're saying they can do. Just the same, the psychologists' conclusion that most people are narcissistic and self-enhancing also suggests, then, that most people have low self-esteem and little to no self-belief, and therefore self-enhance as an unconscious defense. Further, the degree their esteem is low is the degree they self-enhance. This I can certainly agree with.

You can see those concepts from my study playing out in the real world today. Have you ever watched any audition episode of the television show *American Idol* and heard some truly bad singers who believe they're God's gifts to human ears? Some of them were so devastated to hear critical judgments of their singing abilities they became spontaneously enraged and had major emotional breakdowns. I knew several singers who auditioned and were on that show, and they reported those reactions were not produced or dramatized to enhance the entertainment factor of the show. They were real.

Hearing some of those contestants' backgrounds validated my findings that having an unrealistically high sense of yourself is the result of having a low sense of worth and self-belief. Their Adult-Made Minds created false self-belief. I, too, had that kind of deceiving confidence and self-belief early in my life, so I understand it.

I was abused physically and emotionally, bullied, and tormented mercilessly until I was seventeen years old, not only by my peers in school but also by my parents. Let's throw in being sexually molested for four years on top of that as well. Believe me when I say I had no self-esteem as a result and surely "enhanced" my skills and sense of self until I had one profound moment of selflessness and my spiritual transformative event occurred at twenty-eight.

Could you be exaggerating beliefs about yourself that may be getting in your way? Some people outright lie about themselves and all they've done and can do, but they're doing that to compensate. And as they do, they sabotage their manifesting of all they really want.

Now here is that put-you-on-the-spot important question. Do *you* believe in yourself? I mean, really and truly believe in yourself? Don't answer that question until you finish this book. You need time to contemplate that question before you answer. Your immediate answer will probably be coming from your Adult-Made Mind. That son-of-a-gun is fast. So take your time and go deep. Use the barometer graph I gave you to help you with your answer. And don't worry about what you answer. This book is meant to help you fix or enhance whatever your answer is.

# chapter 9

# All You Need Is Love

$\mathcal{U}$p until this point, I've talked about your responsibility in regard to all that you do or do not want to manifest in your life. I told you the key that helps you stop stopping yourself and makes everything you attempt work is unconditional self-belief. By the way, self-belief actually goes hand in hand with self-love. You can't believe in yourself if you don't love yourself, and you can't love yourself if you don't believe in yourself.

I mention that now because it's important to understand their interaction as we discuss relationships in more depth. Whether it's about self-belief or self-love, it's all about the self when it comes to manifesting abundance in rewarding vocation, wellness, and financial security, and attracting loving relationships. As I stated in earlier chapters, it's all about you. However, relationships require more than one "self," more than just you to maintain them. Then how does it work when a relationship requires more than just you?

My claim and evidence so far in this book are that unconditional self-belief makes everything you attempt work. I never suggested there were any exceptions, but what about divine intervention or providence, synchronicity, and coincidence? Where do they come into play in all our manifesting and making things work?

For clarity, synchronicity is occurrences of events that appear significantly related in some way but have no real connection. A coincidence is something significant that happens that doesn't seem to have any cause. Einstein said a coincidence is God's way of remaining anonymous. And providence is some type of guidance from God. The extraordinary point about synchronicity is if the events or circumstances seem related without any obvious reason, this intuitively implies that it was some possibly planned occurrence or destiny.

Metaphysical and spiritual theories propose that our souls predetermine some of the relationships and experiences we will have before each incarnation here. In that way, we get to experience ourselves in the ways we wish. Thus, synchronicities, providence, and coincidences are signs that our plans may be occurring. There's only one roadblock that will get in the way of our original plans once we are here: free will.

Free will is defined by Webster as "the power of acting without the constraint of necessity or fate; the ability to act at one's own discretion." That means that whether you may have set a destiny or blueprint for yourself in this life or divine providence attempts to guide you, the bottom line is you have the choice to follow it all, follow some of it, or create something new altogether. If you believe in yourself enough to let your life unfold, your destiny will take the wheel. However, without self-belief, your AMM and EMM create a new blueprint unconsciously.

For the most part, our Environment-Made Mind and our Adult-Made Mind distract us from our positive plans, and free will permits us to follow the guidance of those minds instead of soul and divine guidance. Why was it so important for me to explain this before I discussed relationships? It's because relationships in conjunction with the Law of Attraction have become highly complicated. Though loving relationships are the most natural systems on Earth, they have become the most dysfunctional and destructive forces here.

You need to fully grasp and accept three crucial concepts about relationships: (1) Attracting any relationship has nothing to do with another person. By means of the Law of Attraction, like attracts like, as I said earlier. Whoever you are on the inside is who you're going to attract into your experience. You know that list you carry titled, "What I Want in a Partner"? Well, cross out "a partner" and write "me" in its place. Be sure you're all the things you want in a partner. (2) Whatever you believe about yourself is going to determine the outcome of the relationship you attract. If you believe you're lovable, the relationship can flourish and last. If you don't believe you're lovable, the relationship can be sabotaged or end disastrously, including in early death. (3) You're only in a relationship to discover more about yourself, not to fulfill your emotional needs or complete you. You're everything you seek already, and a true relationship helps you realize that. The more intimate the relationship, the more you can discover the depths of your true essence.

Whether your soulful plan is to attract a soul you have an arrangement with, maybe your soul mate, or whether you attract a completely different soul in this or any life, your EMM and AMM beliefs will have all to do with the attraction. And as I said, your EMM and AMM beliefs, along with the strength of your soul's mind, also will have everything to do with the direction and outcome of that attraction.

Even though you may draw a relationship that appears to go well in the beginning, your EMM beliefs can bring the worst AMM responses out of each other.

On the other hand, an unstable attraction built on lack and emotional need can still work, depending on the effort you put into it.

While I was a licensed psychotherapist, I did a lot of couples counseling but not the traditional type. My concern wasn't about how each partner was communicating with and listening to the other. My concern was more about how each partner was communicating with and listening to themselves. You know those buttons romantic partners always seem to push that lead to an argument? Those buttons are the beliefs harbored in your Environment-Made Mind, but your Adult-Made Mind always wants to blame your partner, and, voilà, a lover's quarrel!

Paula was a new client who booked an hour reading.

"Hello, Vincent," Paula started. "A good friend of mine referred me to you. She said you were the best."

"Hey, Paula. You have to thank your friend for me for referring you and especially for thinking so highly of me. She's not wrong, but it's nice to hear others admit it," I humorously commented to set a comfortable connection. I went into my opening remarks and instructions and began the reading.

"I have a feeling you made this appointment to talk about your career and direction, but I'm feeling we need to talk about something much more important," I opened.

"You're right. I did want to talk about my job and where I'm going, but what else is so important?" she asked.

"Your relationship or what you think is a relationship," I said refocusing her attention.

"Oh, that," she replied.

"Yes, that! You're married, aren't you?"

"Yes, I am."

"And it's been for some time. About twenty years, correct?" I asked for validation.

"Twenty-one," she stated for accuracy.

"Well, it feels really bland, no communication, distant. Wow! It's as if you're not even married. And I don't believe anything I'm saying is a surprise to you," I concluded.

"It's not. It's been that way for a while now," she confirmed.

"And you made this appointment to talk about your job?" I questioned her seriously.

"I don't think about my marriage much anymore. It is what it is," she stated.

"Yes, Paula. And the world is going to end sometime. It is what it is!" I sarcastically remarked. "But we can all do something to help it while we're here," I added. "Right?"

"I guess so," she answered. I sensed doubt in her voice.

"Paula, as a psychic, I'm telling you, you can do something about it that will make the marriage better. In fact, your souls want you to work on it," I shared.

"We tried. We went to couple counseling and even one of those weekend retreats. It got better for a while and went back to the same old, same old."

"Those weekend retreats are all Band-Aids in my view. They don't heal the issues. They cover them with pretty images, and they distract you from the true concerns. That's why the work didn't last," I explained.

In my almost forty years of doing this work, I've had more women, men, and couples come to me with continued problem relationships who all partook in some types of workshops, counseling, and retreats. Unless you get to the core of the issues, no relationship will work the way it was meant to. And the core of the issues has nothing to do with the couple.

"Paula," I continued, "the issue isn't between you and your husband as a couple. The issue is with each of yourselves as individuals. You don't attract a relationship to complete yourself. You're already complete. That's how you were created. However, you come together as a couple to learn more about yourselves. The more intimate the relationship, the more you learn about who you are. You learn how much more you're capable of loving, of caring, of having compassion. Understanding that *and* realizing that there's no victimization in the world, tell me the biggest complaint you have about your husband in one sentence."

"Oh, wow," Paula started to think. "Well, I say he's become emotionally blank. He doesn't share any emotions, good or bad."

"Okay. That's a good complaint and very common so you know. Now, think about you for a moment. There was a lot of criticism of you in your past, wasn't there?"

"Yes, there was. My—"

"Don't feed me more information," I cut her off quickly. "It was from your mother, wasn't it?"

"Yes, it was. All the time," Paula validated.

"And you felt like you could do nothing right in her eyes," I added. "That must have been very painful for you growing up with that. Here's why that is important for you to recall. How do you believe you coped with that growing up?" I asked her knowing exactly what the answer was.

"I closed off my emotions so it wouldn't bother me," Paula replied as I expected.

"Exactly! Stay with me now. There are two most important things you learn from your parents growing up. The rest you learn from the world. One is whether you're lovable, and the second is how to love yourself. How to love yourself is the pattern you learn from how your parents treated you and the way you responded, and it doesn't have to be a good pattern. You with me so far?" I asked to be sure she was understanding.

"Okay, yeah," Paula responded waiting for the rest.

"Archangel Michael told me you're very self-critical. Isn't that correct?"

"Yes, I am."

"And you also have shut down your emotions so not to continue to feel bad. Actually, what you did is take refuge in your left brain. You're a thinker and not a feeler, right?" I wanted her to admit this out loud.

"You're right. I do think a lot and don't pay attention to my feelings."

"That's right," I came back at her. "Which is why you can live in an emotionless relationship. However, go back to that one-sentence complaint I told you to come up with about your husband. He's become emotionally blank and doesn't share his emotions. Isn't that what you said?" I wanted her to hear her own words.

"I did say that," Paula answered as if she were putting two and two together.

"That's right. And I said you're with another person to learn about yourself, and there's no victimization even in a relationship. So, who do you think you're seeing in the way your husband has been acting toward you?" I wanted her to reflect and answer this question herself so the answer would be more profound.

"Me?" Paula answered slowly as if she wanted to get it right.

"That's right. Good for you. He's reflecting you back to you. You see, if we aren't victims for any reason, then even the way people treat us is influenced by us. Your husband is only mirroring how you treat yourself," I explained.

"Here is the irony about that," I added needing to convey the point. "In order for your husband to be mirroring you, he has similar issues. And because he has similar issues, you can both do similar self-healing work—but together. There's your couples therapy. Read a self-help book together and talk about it. Watch some inspirational movie together and talk about it. Participate in some metaphysical online event together and then talk about it. Attend a New Thought service in person or online, or listen to a spiritual teacher's podcast together and talk about it. Help each other as a team to grow as individuals, and as you do that together, your marriage will grow and flourish beyond your dreams. That is the best couples counseling I can give you and therapy you can both do. You think you can get your husband to do that with you?"

"Maybe. I think I can." Paula sounded unsure.

"Don't approach him as if you're trying to fix him or fix the marriage," I explained. "Tell him you've not been feeling great about yourself, and you really want to do something about it. You want to do some self-improvement work and you were hoping he could help you with that. I really feel strongly that he will participate with you because I feel a wonderful growth and joy in regard to your marriage."

"That's very hopeful. I would love that," Paula replied with hope in her voice.

I finished the reading by giving Paula some more tips and strategies for doing team self-healing work. I reinforced how I saw her marriage and life transforming in the near future and how that transformation was beginning today with her reading. Paula was encouraged and grateful for all I shared.

"Wow!" Paula expressed. "I wasn't expecting that at all. But I'm so grateful you went there. I got more from you in one hour than I got from my therapist in five years."

"Then wait until you see the invoice for my extra fee!" I jokingly replied.

## What Your Relationships Tell You about You

> I would rather trust a woman's instinct than a man's reason.
> —Stanley Baldwin

Let's talk about men and women. Contrary to some religious doctrine, God didn't create man and then woman from man's rib. God created the souls, in its image, as energies. In every religion, including Christianity, there are several references to the pre-existence of the soul before humankind existed. These Bible verses help us understand: "Then shall the dust return to the earth as it was: and the spirit shall return unto God who gave it." (Ecclesiastes 12:7 [KJV 1900]) and "Before I formed thee in the belly I knew thee; and before thou camest forth out of the womb I sanctified thee, and I ordained thee a prophet unto the nations." (Jeremiah 1:5 [KJV])

We were all created before the universe. I have to digress a bit now to lay the foundation of the origins of man and woman. The way Spirit created us was by dividing itself into us. Here we are, all together now as individual energies, each as powerful and bright as the other.

To give a visual image of the creation of souls, picture the sun in the sky as one huge ball of light and energy. Now divide that ball into let's say one hundred smaller balls of light. (That's a random number I chose because I have yet to intuit how many souls God originally created.) By staying together where we were created, all we could see was still one huge ball of light. We never saw our own individual lights, so the intelligence, God, had an idea (again, conjecture, though supported by a lot of psychic guidance and messages): "Let's together now create a place where you can each go to discover and see your own lights and power."

And, thus, the universes began. Yes, there's more than one universe. And, yes, there's more than just this universe with incarnated souls living there, but that's another book I'll be writing.

Earth and our universe serve our purpose for discovering ourselves and our divinity. However, once the physical planets and such appeared, we wanted a physical form to embody to live here. Hence, we formed these bodies as co-creators using the force and power of Spirit. Originally, we created nongender-specific bodies. We were androgenous—"having the characteristics or nature of both male and female" (*Merriam-Webster*). You might want to read stories about the civilization of Lemuria, our pre-existence before modern humans.

As we continued to discover ourselves, the city of Atlantis developed, where we really messed up. Both aren't necessarily factual places; however, they are stories to explain our human development, different from the scientific theories of evolution. And, by the way, our original understanding of human evolution proposed by Darwin was based on his observations of the fruit fly. Well-known scientists and experts are currently disproving those theories. Read *Fractal Time* by Gregg Braden. He shares mind-blowing evidence that throws a wrench in all the school-taught evolution theories.

According to various written and oral stories about Atlantis, we destroyed ourselves by misusing the power of the sun and energy of the earth we figured out how to harness. It was like letting a whole bunch of children loose in Toys "R" Us without any adult supervision. We quickly tapped into our divine abilities but without the maturity to handle them.

Going forward, what I'm about to share with you now is my own insightful and psychic information about what happened next. There was nothing to pull us back from the slippery slope we were going down while in Atlantis. The two greatest gifts God gave our souls upon creation to help us grow and evolve were intuition and intellect. When we originally created the first physical vehicle for the soul, both our intuition and intellect were contained in the same unit. The trouble started when we had intuitive feelings to guide us with our choices and our intellect began talking us out of those feelings. We quickly became conflicted with the inner messages.

Once we destroyed our first physical existence, our souls concluded we needed to do it differently. My conjecture is that the Earthly souls gathered in the heavenly dimension after our physical destruction to develop a new plan on how to live incarnate in this new physical world. We figured we needed to preserve both our intuition and our intellect since they were both necessary to survive and thrive. So this is how I hear the discussion going:

"What if we take our two greatest abilities and put them in two different physical bodies? We can give each body both intuition and intellect, but in one body give more intuition and the other body more intellect. That way if the body with more intuition isn't following their intuitive guidance, then the body with the more intellect can help. And if the body with the more intellect isn't following their intellectual guidance, then the body with the more intuition can help. Doing it like this, if we're screwing up again, we won't lose both abilities at the same time because one or the other can help stop us. And we'll make it natural for the physical beings to be drawn to each other to help each other grow and understand their powers slowly so we don't abuse them again."

This is the story of how the male and female came into existence that developed within my psychic sense over the past almost forty years. Thus, the Bible's story of Adam and of Eve being split from Adam was the symbolic story of the formation of those new life forms.

This was just the foundation of how we decided to survive in a physical existence. After splitting the original humanoid, however it appeared, all sorts of issues developed from there that I will go into in another book sometime in the future. For now, it was necessary for me to share this with you to help you understand the functioning of all relationships—family, acquaintance, friendship, couple, intimate, and marriage. We all come together to learn about ourselves through our relationships.

As I reflected to Paula, she hadn't been paying attention to the way she was treating herself until I made her define how her husband was treating her. Once she did that, she clearly saw her husband was mirroring her own lack of emotional connection with herself. And once she recognized that, she knew that her husband and marriage would greatly benefit from the work they could do together. *Transform* is the word I like to use.

Six months later, Paula *and* her husband Jim made an appointment with me to ask me about their moving plans and to also share how much they had grown and how their marriage had *transformed*. They shared how they read books, watched movies, attended seminars online, and constantly talked with each other now. Jim expressed that once he started talking about all that was pent up inside him, he felt the world lift from his shoulders. He said he never wanted to burden Paula with all his shit, which was why he never talked with her about what he was feeling. He thanked me for what I had told Paula during her first reading.

"We were headed for a divorce, and I thought Paula didn't love me anymore because she stopped talking with me. You saved our marriage, Vincent," Jim said.

"Oh, no, I didn't save your marriage," I rebutted. "You and Paula did. Good for you for being open enough and willing enough to do the work. You see, contrary to what your father used to tell you (I threw in a psychic message), you *are* good enough, Jim."

"Yeah, well you got us started," he added.

"That's because I'm damn good at what I do, Jim, and so are you and Paula."

Look at all your relationships today, especially your most intimate ones. What may they be telling you about you? What haven't you paid attention to that is being manifested in the way others are treating you? Don't be afraid to go there. I know many relationships can be abusive and hurtful, and, therefore, what I've said here may hurt you more. It's difficult to accept that you're the cause of how others treat you. However, think what that really means. It means you have the power to change how you're being treated in the world. That's right. And that's an empowering belief to grasp and fix in your mind.

I never said this book was going to make you feel good as you read it. I said that if you *did* read it, you would gain the understanding and the tools to release and heal the pains and resistances, break the sabotaging thoughts and patterns, stop stopping yourself, finally gain the key to make everything you attempt work, so you can become unstoppable.

# chapter 10

## The Trouble with Angels

*Y*our Adult-Made Mind is incredible at masking your issues. You may have a pleasant personality and life with a fairly functional family, beautiful friends, an adoring lifelong partner, and loving children and not know you're still stopping yourself from having more.

Maybe you have a job you truly enjoy, but it goes nowhere. Maybe your finances are adequate, though you still must budget and be careful not to splurge. Maybe you're fairly healthy as per the blood tests and routine doctor visits, but your physical stamina and strength aren't as optimal as your desired activity level. Maybe you know most people genuinely like you and you have many friends, but you have no idea the impact you have on their lives or if they truly care about you. Maybe you're also generally happy.

If this is you, as great as your life may sound, something you're doing or not doing is still getting in the way of creating total fulfillment and joy for yourself. If you're able to manifest at least that much in your life, think of how much more you can create if you remove whatever block or blocks you may have.

It's important I share the story of a client, Eileen, I mentored for a year to give you an example of the different effects the EMM and AMM (Environment-Made Mind and Adult-Made Mind) can have on you. The lack of self-belief can be so hidden and your AMMs so creative that neither you nor the world would ever be the wiser.

Eileen experienced a lot of hurt in her youth from her parents' divorce. At ten years old, Eileen accidentally overheard her father talking on the phone with his mistress. She understood what was going on, and it was Eileen who informed her mother of his affair, which resulted in their divorce. That caused Eileen great pain because she blamed herself for breaking up her family. That, along with Eileen getting teased about her extra weight in school, caused many EMM beliefs as well. When she matured and her AMM formed to protect her from her Environment-Made Mind beliefs, her defenses became so strong it took almost forty-eight years for her to discover her true maladaptive self-beliefs. They were so repressed and suppressed she could never identify them. Interestingly, the defenses she formed served her well, although she manifested what she really desired only modestly throughout her life.

Eileen was able to attract a passionate and loving partner, who unfortunately also experienced many childhood hurts. Remember I said like attracts like. She married him at twenty-two years old, and, between the two of them, they were able to manifest beautiful blessings working off each other's passions and beliefs.

Eileen's personality was angelic. Where others may have only cared about being loved, all Eileen cared about was being lovable. And she was. Everyone who met Eileen loved Eileen, and they still do. To compensate for feeling like she broke her family, her motivation in her life became to fix everything. She became genuinely caring, compassionate, empathetic, and, most of all, loving and accepting of everyone. She always saw everyone's goodness before their badness. Nevertheless, her untapped EMM emotions and beliefs eventually caught up to her and resulted in health issues.

You may be asking what types of influences your AMM defenses might develop. In an earlier chapter, I told you the two most important aspects you learn from your parents are whether you're lovable and how to love yourself. The way they treat you growing up is how you decipher whether you're lovable or not and how you end up treating yourself as an adult. Remember I said that? Well, the way they treat you also influences the types of defenses your AMM creates. Some parents were overly critical and treated their children harshly. The outcome was that those children became adults who treated not only themselves harshly and critically but also treated others harshly and critically.

Also, the extent of the disparaging EMM beliefs you harbor from the abuse and torment you may have experienced during your youth will be the extent your AMM beliefs can be self-destructive. You've read, heard, and seen so much of the horrible things people have done to themselves and others over the past several years alone. So many became aggressive and self-protective even though they may have begun as deeply loving souls. These people harbored so much hurt and so many painful Environment-Made Mind beliefs that they lashed out at the world.

There are those who experienced similar torments but whose personas are to be nice to everyone, walk around confidently, keep themselves looking perfect, quickly form deep emotional friendships, and act in comical ways to make people laugh. These souls would never lash out at others, only at themselves.

The opposite was true for Eileen growing up. Her mom, who had her own issues that eventually caused her early death, was a warm-hearted and friendly person to everyone and never harsh to her children. She may have been passive-aggressive and used guilt to get what she wanted from her kids, but she was never cruel to them. That was the pattern Eileen learned and why she was never harsh or cruel to herself or others. Thus, her AMM defenses were to make herself as kind and lovable as she could, even though deep down she did not believe she was. This most certainly worked well for her, which brings up a new point that is also important to understand.

Just because you develop AMM defenses that are attempting to protect you from negative EMM beliefs, those defenses aren't always negative. Some people's defenses are obviously negative and self-destructive like those people who lash out at others or are angry at the world all the time. Their defenses developed that way maybe because their environments were filled with hatred, prejudice, rage, alcoholism, violence, or any other severe negative behavior.

On the other extreme, there are those like Eileen, whose defenses make them loving, caring, and kind because their AMMs were influenced by their seemingly more positive environments. Then there are those people in the middle who are good-natured, self-sacrificing, and always doing for others. Their AMM defenses may have been influenced by having to work so hard as kids to gain any attention and affection, so they treat themselves the same, believing they need to work so hard.

Recall that I said everything created in your AMM is fake and false. Thus, all your AMM behaviors, bad or good, are false and fake. They're not coming from the genuine you. Your EMM feelings are more genuine because that's what you really believe about yourself. That's why apparently good and happy people can also stop themselves and claim it's not working. They're only acting and pretending to be good without truly believing they are.

Those people who are self-sacrificing and always doing for other people are never emotionally fulfilled because no one can possibly give to them what they need. Most likely, their EMM belief is that they are so unworthy they have to earn love. Thus, their AMM defenses become pleasing others and being endearing, even at their own expense. Consequently, their lack of self-worth manifests constant lack of reciprocation, betrayal, and heartbreak by the people they thought were their dearest friends.

But there's hope. You may have created wonderful AMM defenses that aren't sincerely who you believe you are, but that doesn't mean you're not that person you're pretending to be. I know that sounds like a complete contradiction but go back and reread the foundation chapters about the EMM and AMM and how they are the layers blocking your true essence in your super-conscious and soul minds.

Just like Eileen, people can really hide behind those AMM defenses and never know they are causing their own blocks. No one ever questions their self-beliefs, including them, because they carry themselves so confidently. That's why most people through lifetime after lifetime stop themselves and never know why they can't get universal principles to work for them so they can experience all of who they are. They hide their lack of self-belief so well.

And when you get to the other side beyond the veil in the spirit realm, all the answers aren't fed to you there either. Highly evolved beings understand the benefits of discovering your own answers. Even in the mental health arena, psychotherapists believe it's much more powerful for people to come up with answers to their issues on their own. That's why therapy can go on for twelve years or longer. I say bullshit to that. It's taking too damn long for all of us to figure it out for ourselves, with too much pain and suffering in between.

I believe, therefore, that I was awakened and inspired to do the work I do and write this book to give you the answers I discovered. Even with the answer at hand, you're still the one who has to accept it and apply it for yourself in order for it to work. Besides, there's nothing you can come up with on your own, ever. It's all been created already either by you or God, and it's just waiting in the cosmos for you to manifest into this experience.

Eileen hid her lack of self-belief incredibly well. For the longest time, not even the smallest Environment-Made Mind belief snuck its way through to her conscious mind—even when she got into fights with her husband. She was never consciously worried about whether anyone loved her. Nevertheless, her EMM and AMM surfaced, though still behind the scenes, working vigorously to keep her from creating a truly rewarding and joyful life.

With all the love Eileen received from others throughout her life, she never truly felt lovable but didn't know that until we did our work together. You see, you can't feel or give to others what you don't feel and give to yourself—period. So how can so many people say they love their children, their friends, their parents, or their partners so much, sometimes even more than themselves?

We're capable of loving from the head and not from the heart. However, that's a thinking love and not a feeling love. There's a difference. Have you ever heard someone, especially a man, who is completely left brained say I love you? It's difficult to believe them because there's no genuine emotion backing up the words. That's one reason so many children end up believing they are unlovable— even having parents who expressed the words all the time.

That is an extreme example of obvious head love. Many times, though, it's not as perceptible because all your other personality traits can be so emotionally driven. With head love, we can convince ourselves that it's genuine love we are giving and feeling for others. As subtle as the differences between head and heart love may seem, they aren't. The differences are major though not easy to admit.

How can you tell where your love is coming from? Well, you can read the Bible verse "Love is . . ." (Corinthians 13: 4-8) and the poems written from this verse to see how you measure up. However, it says more about what love isn't and what love does rather than what love is.

Christianity tried to define love through the story and example of Jesus. Paraphrasing, God loved us so much that he "sacrificed" his only begotten son to save us from our sins. Really? The only way to show you love someone is through sacrifice? That was truly a human idea and not one from a loving deity. Love has nothing to do with sacrificing anything. Sacrifice by definition means giving up something valued for the sake of something else regarded as more important or worthy.

Seriously? God believed we were more worthy than Jesus, so having him crucified was the only way to forgive us of our sins? Ideas like this are why it's so hard for us to love ourselves. That was actually a head-love rationalization and example.

Heartfelt love never feels the need for sacrifice. It feels only a willingness to give without a need to give up anything or get anything in return. Here's the irony of what I just said. Though heart love requires nothing in return, the more we give it freely, the more we receive it tenfold in return.

Contrarily, love from your head isn't sustaining; it's brittle; it doesn't allow you to manifest all you deserve. It keeps you from recognizing the truth, and it doesn't give you the strength to stand for divine values. That's why, convinced you're a loving person, you can abandon your brother and sister souls here when they need you most and be a hypocrisy of goodness and love rather than an example of these qualities. Also, because it's not real love, head love can cause you to feel betrayed and hurt by others. It's not unconditional. Unfortunately, there's very little real love on Earth. If there were, it would be so much easier to experience, and we all would be so much stronger. We are all very much still aspiring to that.

People will see your AMM defenses way before you ever do without realizing that's what they are seeing. The way they respond to you is based on how you present yourself, and how they interpret what they're seeing. People with positive AMM defenses like Eileen will intuitively recognize your AMM defenses are the false you. Now, they may not be able to verbalize what your AMM beliefs are or why you have them, but they will sense the way you're acting isn't you. Maybe you've experienced that sometime in your life. Think about anytime a friend or family member said something like, "That's not you. That's not who you are."

Opposite that are the negative people who will without a doubt misinterpret your words and behaviors because of their own AMM beliefs. For example, some negative people thought Eileen was acting nice just to get attention. But Eileen saw through everyone's defenses except her own. She also saw through people's Environment-Made Mind beliefs and into their souls. Eileen was able to see the God and greatness within people and still does. My work with her was to help her see the God and greatness within herself and how she was empowering others.

Eileen sought out my guidance as a mentor because one day while attending her spiritual center's meditation workshop, she had a profound vision and epiphany. While doing a guided meditation, she saw herself as a twelve-year-old child sitting on her backyard swing all alone one day; she felt very sad because she was alone and believed no one loved her.

When she came out of the meditation, she was in tears realizing for the first time in her life that she never believed she was lovable and that all her friends, family, and husband really didn't love her. Eileen had suppressed those beliefs and feelings for over forty-eight years. Because of those hidden beliefs, she stopped herself from truly thriving.

Our work together for only one year proved to be deeply rewarding for Eileen, for her and her husband's lives have exploded with joyful manifestations and so many more deserved blessings. The work wasn't easy for Eileen because her Environment-Made Mind and Adult-Made Mind beliefs and defenses were so strong and so ingrained within her psyche that she would occasionally lose sight of how little Eileen was still influencing big Eileen's life. However, her work and commitment to herself proved to be well worth her efforts. Eileen admitted to me during our last session together that she kept the mantra I gave her pasted around her house so she could see it all the time.

"I love myself so much that I'm going to do whatever I need to do in order to experience my greatest existence here on Earth because I deserve it!" she said.

Are you willing to go that deep and do the most profound work you could ever do to love yourself and finally face your EMM beliefs and AMM defenses even if you're the most loved person around but not yet living a life that matches that? If you answer a loud and firm "Yes!" you know why you were drawn to reading this book.

# chapter 11

## Turn on Your Heat and Bake Your Cake

*I*n sharing the stories of a few of my clients with you, I am able to illustrate some of the internal damaging beliefs people have that stop them from manifesting a more fruitful life. I also explain how those beliefs develop from an early age by the negative messages received from the environment and stored in a new part of the mind, the Environment-Made Mind that the brain creates to house them.

Then I demonstrate the formation and development of the Adult-Made Mind, which creates a new set of beliefs to shield and protect the conscious mind from the painful ones in the EMM. And while you're trying to tap into the power of the Law of Attraction to create the life you want and deserve, the anomalies going on in your own mind are stopping you and even creating what you don't want.

And don't forget the same forces at play in your mind make you think you believe in and love yourself when you really don't, so, of course, most of what you attempt to do to thrive doesn't work or works only to a limited extent. As I mentioned, without believing in yourself, no matter what self-help or spiritual principles you apply, it's almost impossible to get anything to work.

Now I'm going to tell you how to get it all working again. It's actually an easy process. All you have to do is face your AMMs and EMMs. That's right. Just face and admit the feelings and beliefs you've been holding onto, and your life will begin to work for you. You might be saying right now, "Oh, that's all I have to do, Vincent, is face my EMM and AMM beliefs? You make it sound so easy." I said the process is simple. The *practice* is difficult.

I'm sure sometime in your life you had a nightmare where someone or something was chasing you. You were trying to run away, but you couldn't because you could hardly move your legs in your dream. Something was stopping them from moving. Maybe you were trying to scream and you couldn't because no matter how hard you tried to speak or yell, nothing would come out except some moaning.

Dream specialists say you can learn how to stop running away in your dream and face and confront what's chasing you. If you do, you can actually learn what is unconsciously and emotionally bothering you. That threatening character is a part of you—a fear, a negative belief or attitude, or some destructive behavior. You actually can learn to control your dreams. That's what's known as lucid dreaming. If you do confront whatever is threatening you in a dream, you actually disempower it.

Many people who have a lot of painful beliefs within their EMMs that were suppressed by their AMMs have nightmares often. Some include scenes where they are standing near raging waters, like an ocean with massive waves crashing up against a rocky shore. Water in all dreams represents your emotions. The dreamers are always fearful in those dreams that the waves are going to wash them from the shore, and they will drown. That clearly was about the dreamers' fear that their emotions are going to overpower them and something life-threatening will happen.

I myself had healing work to do from all the emotional, physical, and sexual abuse I experienced until I was seventeen years old. I used to have frequent nightmares with raging waters. After doing the healing work I will be sharing, I had a dream one night where I was standing on a beautiful beach with blue skies. The sun was shining, but suddenly a gigantic wave was coming right toward me on the beach. My heart started racing as it always did in dreams like that.

Just as I was about to turn and run, I said, "No. I'm going to face that wave." I turned toward the wave, took a deep breath, and the wave went over me, and then I was standing under the water with my eyes closed. I held my breath for as long as I could, and finally with courage I opened my eyes and took a deep breath while under the water. I didn't drown and the wave disappeared, the water became calm, and I remained standing on the shore enjoying the view. I actually smiled and said, "I'm okay."

When I woke in the morning, any anxiety I might have had the day before was gone. In fact, I never feared my emotions again. I allowed myself to feel them all, knowing they would no longer get the best of me. I stopped suppressing them.

Dreams like the one I described are examples of the psychological understanding that if you face whatever scares you the most, you can resolve it. Some of our greatest spiritual leaders gave testimony to the same principle. One of the first was Jesus. He said, "Ye have heard that it hath been said, an eye for an eye, and a tooth for a tooth: But I say unto you, that ye resist not evil: but whosoever shall smite thee on thy right cheek, turn to him the other also." (Matthew 5:38–39 [KJV])

Jesus was saying not to fight back because that would be evil as well. But he was saying even more than that with these words. If he just meant for you not to fight back, he would have said to walk away if someone "smites" you. Instead, he said to turn the other cheek. That also suggests standing there right in front of the assailant. In other words, stand and confront that which is threatening you. When you do that, the assaulter is forced to face his or her own inhumanity. In doing so, the assaulter backs down and the threat no longer exists.

Mahatma Gandhi is considered another great spiritual leader who shows us that we should not only treat each other with peace and love but offer ourselves the same. He was an example of peaceful resistance, and his leadership and example gained India its independence from British rule. Gandhi always stood in resistance to British law over his people. And there were many times the British tried to beat him down physically, but he always took his stance, literally, opposing them. He knew when you face the menace with peace and love in your heart, the threat will back down, and it did. Eventually, India became a free nation. So how does this relate to your AMM and EMM?

Let's recall that the reason you have your AMM is to protect and shield you from the painful beliefs you developed from the conscious and unconscious negative messages you received from your environment during your youth. They're harbored in your EMM. And together, your EMM and AMM are blocking the knowing truth of your divinity and unlimited ability that resides in your soul's mind. The greatest threats you have, therefore, are the painful beliefs and memories in your EMM. You must extinguish their power over you. And as I said, you have to face your threats in order to disempower them.

Many of you will say, "I've been doing a lot of therapy and self-improvement work to rid myself of past issues, and it's still not working." You may have been, but may I remind you that if it's still not working, you were or are doing that work from your AMM and not your EMM. Freud developed the psychoanalytical model of psychotherapy because he knew the importance of getting through the defenses and to the root cause of a person's issues in order for any therapy to work.

That model of treatment, of course, took a long time because Freud believed you needed to examine and analyze each trauma and painful experience to resolve it. That turned off many people who needed therapy and discouraged new therapists from doing that work. So new psychologists developed simpler models of therapy to help people "cope" better in life, but that totally excluded the metaphysical understanding of manifesting and the Law of Attraction. Remember, coping only allows you to survive, not create.

Where Freud was correct in his model, however, was the understanding you need to actually face your inner fears rather than just intellectualize them. If just hearing the cause of why you have not been able to create the life you want was enough, then you should be able to put this book down and create right now. You can't. Hearing isn't enough. The message must get down to your heart. Just like love must come from your heart, belief must come from there as well. Your heart is governed by your soul, and your soul resides beneath your EMM and AMM. The first step in getting to your soul is to face your first threat, your AMM defenses, and then your second and most painful, your EMM beliefs.

I would like to share a Disney story that is a perfect visual depiction of what I assert here. I believe Walt Disney was a spiritual man with great insight and intuition. His work was extremely inspiring for both young and old. He knew that whatever animated movie he was going to create, the adults would be accompanying their children to see the movie, so each movie he chose had moral values for the children and possibly metaphysical values for the adults.

For example, *Snow White and the Seven Dwarfs* could well be a metaphor for your seven chakras (the seven dwarfs), your divine feminine (Snow White), and your divine masculine (Prince Charming). When your divine feminine and masculine are out of balance, your chakras act chaotically, like Bashful, Dopey, Sneezy, Sleepy, Doc, Grumpy, and Happy. However, when they are connected and working harmoniously, everyone lives happily ever after.

I believe *The Lion King* is a metaphysical story about our relationship with God and ourselves and how we all went off the path and what we need to do to get back on the path again. That's why this story is perfect for this book.

It begins with Mufasa as the king of Pride Rock, and as long as he was king, all life at Pride Rock was in perfect balance and harmony with an abundance of everything needed. Mufasa represents God, your higher consciousness, and as long as God within you rules your life, everything remains in balance and harmony, and you experience nothing but abundance. Life is as it's supposed to be. Mufasa has a brother, Scar, perfectly named. Scar is envious of Mufasa, and he wants to be king. Scar represents all the pains life can have and the "scars" they leave behind. They can become overwhelming and want to control your life. In the movie Scar is always trying to overpower Mufasa, but Mufasa always wins out. Even with the pains of life, if you keep your path in the light, the God within will always win out.

So now, Mufasa and Sarabi, the masculine and feminine of God, have a child, Simba. Simba represents all of us, God's children. And while Simba is a child growing up, Scar tries to get to Mufasa by tempting Simba to make the wrong choices. Through your youth, your negative experiences and pains, EMM and AMM beliefs can distract you from who you really are and pull you away from the God within. Eventually, Scar causes Mufasa's death.

When you let your EMM beliefs get out of control, your pains and torments cause you to completely lose sight of the God within you, thus separating from and killing God off. Feeling guilty now, Simba leaves everyone and runs away from Pride Rock. In life, not wanting to deal with the pains and guilt from all the hurt because you blame yourself for everything, you create your AMM and defenses to hide and suppress those feelings.

While Simba has left Pride Rock, he finds Timon and Pumba who teach Simba about *hakuna matata*, "no worries." Just live carefree as if nothing is wrong. For a while, this distracts Simba as he grows into an adult with seemingly no worries. You can create such powerful defenses in your AMM, you can think everything is okay, and you never acknowledge the anguish that still lies deep within.

One day, Simba is at unrest with himself, feeling there is more to him than who he has become. At that same time, Nala, Simba's childhood girlfriend, finds Simba after searching for him for a long time. Nala represents your divine feminine and intuition, and in letting your AMM defenses down even just a bit, your soul's mind can make its way through to consciousness, and you can briefly hear your connection with God and your insights.

Nala tries to remind Simba who he is as the king and that he needs to take his rightful place at Pride Rock. She tells him that since he has left, Scar has taken over and Pride Rock has fallen into disarray. Your intuition is always trying to remind you that you're connected to God, and by remaining disconnected you manifest lack rather than abundance in all you attempt.

Even after Nala talks with Simba, he still doesn't listen and go back. He's too afraid. Even when your soul reminds you of the truth of who you are, your EMM pains can be so strong and AMM defenses so controlling that you can still ignore your greatest inner guidance, convincing yourself you're making the right choices. After Nala leaves, Simba cries out to his father, asking why Mufasa isn't there for Simba as Mufasa promised. It's at your lowest state of mind you usually seek your highest help.

From nowhere, Rafiki, the baboon and the spiritual leader of Pride Rock, finds Simba. If you genuinely seek the God within even when you feel the furthest away, God will send a way for you to find It. Rafiki tells Simba his father is still alive, and he can see him anytime he wants. Rafiki represents your connection with your higher self, which never left the heavenly dimensions.

In Christianity, your sacred connection is the same as the Holy Spirit we all supposedly lost when Adam and Eve first sinned. Symbolically, Christianity was correct but not because man sinned. When Simba ran away because he felt guilt from his behaviors, he left and lost Rafiki. When you hide in your AMM, you lose that connection, that holy connection to the God force.

Before continuing, you need to watch one of the most powerful scenes in the entire movie. Go to YouTube and search for the video "Mufasa's Ghost: The Lion King," and it will take you to the four-minute clip from the movie. Once you watch it, come back and continue reading.

I bet you never saw *The Lion King* that way before. You need to watch the entire movie with this understanding, and it will take on a whole new experience for you. In that scene, you heard two profound statements from Mufasa. "You have forgotten who you are and so you have forgotten me." God is telling his children we have forgotten our connection with him because we have forgotten our own divinity and magnificence. Basically, we stopped believing in ourselves. When you disconnect from your Godness, you forget who you are. Once you forget who you are, you forget you were God.

Then he continues, "You are more than what you have become. Remember who you are. You are my son and the one true king." God is saying, "You are my child and the one true God." Where have we heard that story before? Maybe the Jesus story? Remember, Simba represents all of us, not just one of us.

For the rest of the story, Simba goes back to fight Scar and all Scar's allies. Once he wins over Scar, Simba takes his rightful place as king and puts Pride Rock back in its proper order and balance and filled with abundance. You can interpret that.

You may be thinking, "But, Vincent, this is only a cartoon and not reality. It's not as easy as that." Actually, Simba has to fight a lot of darkness and enemies before he gets to take over as king. You, too, will have difficult times when you face your threats and inner demons. I said the process is easy, but the practice is difficult. But you, too, will win if you face your threats.

During this process of turning your heat on and starting to believe in yourself, you must realize negative feelings aren't detriments to your work. Negative feelings are necessary because they signal you as to a negative belief or thought you may have. Unresolved negative beliefs and thoughts are detrimental. Resolving the bad feelings begins the procedure for turning the belief and thought around. Thus, your emotions aren't what are blocking you from developing true self-belief. Your AMM defenses are. So first you need to recognize and admit that you have some fairly controlling AMM beliefs.

You have to be willing to first face your defenses. Sometimes, your AMM is so convincing, and it has to be in order to work, that you may not even recognize you have any defenses. I have so many clients who at first tell me they're really happy and have great lives, similar to what Angie told me in my first story, "Oh, I have a great life. I'm happy doing what I want. My childhood was wonderful. I had great, loving parents." And they tell me this before I even have a chance to say anything to them. Of course, while they're telling me this, my bullshit monitor from my psychic ability keeps going off. With one such recent in-person appointment, with Jill, the session went like this:

I started. "I'm feeling there's strife between you and your partner. You're married, right?"

"Yes, I am, and it was terrible with him not too long ago. He was very abusive. But it's better than it was before, so I'm happy," Jill quickly added.

"So, you're saying you're happy with your marriage then?" I asked quite doubtful because of my sense.

"Oh, God, no, but like I said it's better than it was," she tried to clarify.

"So, compared to it being real crappy, it's not as crappy is what you're saying?"

"Yes."

"And you're happy with that," I stated to reflect her responses.

"Oh, no. I'm still thinking of leaving him. I'm just happy it's better than it was."

"I'm also feeling you had deep problems with your father, but you said your parents were very loving."

"Well, they treated me better than they treated each other. Dad was very abusive to Mom, but once he left, it was better. I knew they loved me."

"How did you know that?" I was really questioning her self-awareness at this point.

"Like I said, they never treated me the way they treated each other. Dad tried to use me against Mom, but it never worked. Mom was strong and she would keep me from seeing Dad if he acted up." Jill responded without any negative emotions.

"I'm also seeing problems with your health," I went on.

"Oh, yes, but it's much better now since I'm on pain meds. I don't feel all that horrible pain unless I forget to take my meds," she nonchalantly answered.

"And you say you're completely happy with your life now and know you had a happy childhood," I summed up her replies.

"Oh, yes, I do. Why do you keep asking me that? Don't you think I'm happy and had a great childhood?" she asked with great confusion.

The exchange went on like this throughout the session until I stopped her. The entire time Jill was telling me about her "wonderful" life and childhood, her eyes were wandering all over the place. When she talked about the troubles she was experiencing, she looked me straight in the eyes. When I shared what I saw that countered Jill's beliefs, she became completely confused. In her mind, she was completely happy, but the outcome of her life was about actual unhappiness.

You might ask why not just leave Jill to her beliefs if she thinks she's happy? I'll answer that this way. Voltaire was a famous French philosopher and writer in the eighteenth century. He was considered among the most enlightened writers of France. He posed an interesting philosophical question that people needlessly still debate today. While pursuing my psychology degree in 1997, we debated this exact Voltaire question in my philosophy class. His philosophical question was whether it is better to be totally ignorant but completely happy or totally all-knowing and completely unhappy. Think about that for a moment. What would you answer?

Here's the correct answer that few individuals ever get. It's a bogus question with no answer. If you were completely ignorant, you wouldn't know you were happy; therefore, you couldn't be. And if you were all-knowing, you would know how to create happiness and you would be. Besides this question being a fallacy, you can't pose everything as being either/or.

The actual valid question is this: would you rather be all-knowing and completely happy or ignorant and not know whether you're happy or unhappy? Of course, the answer is obvious. Therefore, is it best, then, to cover your misery with ignorance of it and create a fake happiness that you couldn't truly feel anyway? Remember love from your head versus love from your heart? This is the same thing: happiness from your head.

I used this one client and philosophical question to stress two important points. First, your AMM can create an ignorance-like illusion to keep you from recognizing and feeling your negative emotions. As a result, you will manifest more of what you don't want. Second, all your suppressed and repressed negative emotions will turn into an illness eventually even if you're convinced you're happy.

Rest assured when I work privately with clients, I do burst bubbles and get to the truth. You know when you get a blister over a burn or infection sometimes? You can't get the healing ointment directly on the infection because the blister is covering it as the body's own protection. Well, sometimes you just have to pop that blister to get the ointment directly on the burn or infection. I pop a lot of blisters.

Use your life to learn what it is you need to face in your AMM. Again, this may be painful because you may have to admit to beliefs you might not like, especially if it's been serving you well. I remind you that you're responsible for all you manifest in your life, including your dad leaving all his money to your "bitch" sister.

Assess some of your current beliefs and behaviors. Do you blame others in any way for your lack? That could include blaming family, friends, your romantic partner, society, or, yes, the government. You saw a lot of that AMM defense during the 2016 presidential election in the United States. There was blame placed on Muslims, illegal immigrants, Mexicans, refugees, LBGTQ+s, the media, and President Obama.

What fears do you think you reasonably have about losing something vital or loved? All fears stem from your Environment-Made Mind and aren't reasonable. Therefore, if you think you have a just fear, then that is an Adult-Made Mind defense. What are your prej-udices, self-destructive behaviors, unforgivable feel-ings, angers, resentments, human phobias, or apathies? They're all defenses.

You're strong enough to face them, and as you do they will weaken in strength and begin to fade. The AMM can only create defenses you're willing to accept. You might say to yourself, "Okay, I'm acknowledging that my AMM defenses have been hiding what I really feel and believe about the world and myself. And because of that, I've not been able to manifest all I want and deserve. I'm telling the Universe, which includes my soul, to show me all my AMM defenses. I'm ready and willing to face them."

That will certainly get the ball rolling. "Seek and ye shall find" goes a long way and helps in all areas of your life. As your AMM becomes disempowered, you will begin to feel your EMM emotions and memories. When you do, just allow yourself to feel them. There's a saying in the field of psychology: "You need to feel in order to heal." We are so afraid to feel our emotions because we think we're going to break. We don't know how to cope with them, which is why the AMM formed originally.

As beings we just hate feeling bad. The trick to reduce all bad feelings is to believe in yourself. The more you do, the fewer bad feelings you will experience. You will manifest more positive than negative circumstances, and the negatives will roll off you without leaving scars or residuals. I can attest to that wholeheartedly.

This is an easy way to face what your EMM dogmas may be. If you're not in a rewarding vocation or pursuing a dream, you may believe, "I'm not capable enough." If you're struggling financially or aren't as financially abundant as you'd like to be, you believe, "I'm not deserving enough." If you aren't healthy, you may believe, "I'm not worthy enough." If you aren't in a loving relationship right now, I know you believe, "I'm not lovable." All these beliefs caused you to stop believing in and loving yourself and creating the life you want. As you face them, you will disempower them as well. As you disempower them, your self-belief will begin to return.

Think about this for a minute. Your AMMs were created by your adult mind, so they sound reasonable and mature, while your EMMs were created by your immature mind and sound childish and unreasonable. By repeating your EMM beliefs out loud, you will admit they sound silly: "I don't have enough money because I don't deserve to have money." "I don't have a lover in my life because I'm just not lovable."

Now, unless you're really in bad shape and truly believe those things, you'll feel silly saying them. But that's exactly what you believe. And say this out loud too: "I don't believe in myself or love myself." That sounds bad when you speak it, but it's true.

Facing your AMM and EMM lets you see what needs to be healed. The healing starts from the moment you acknowledge what needs to be healed. You know you're doing the correct work because, as you just start it, your life begins to transform. More synchronicities occur right away, and you just start manifesting more of what you want. And there will always be signs along the way to validate your work. That's where the saying, "God helps those who help themselves," comes in. Your soul's mind and God within will do everything to reinforce your genuine work.

Chances are you've already done some work on yourself. Face it, most of us had some type of story that caused some maladaptive beliefs. Even if you've done work, you worked on the issues the pains may have caused. The reason you still don't have true self-belief, then, is because of the scars. I mentioned before that all injuries cause scars. Although you may heal the symptoms and results of the injuries, you rarely get rid of all the scars. So even when you are experiencing the best events in your life, one of those scars can rear its ugly head and botch it all up for you. You weren't paying attention, so it got the best of you by influencing the Law of Attraction. That's why the character Scar was a perfect name for that character in *The Lion King*. And remember, just when you think you've done all the work you can do, you haven't.

# chapter 12

## You Gotta Love Magic Tricks

*I* always loved magic tricks because they're fascinating illusions. I used to have a magic kit when I was younger but didn't continue improving the tricks as I got older. I should've kept at it because I would've impressed the hell out of my grandchildren. I did show them corny grandpa tricks I made up when they were toddlers, but they stopped being fooled quickly.

My interest in magic never waned though. I just redirected it to the real magic of life and our ability to manifest. My desire became creating magic tricks that could transform a person's life. I consider disempowering your Adult-Made Mind and releasing those Environment-Made Mind beliefs pretty magical. That certainly produces miracles. I also developed other tools that have magical results.

I already shared one such tool earlier called the Three R System. The first R is for *review*. Review your innermost beliefs and thoughts. Be willing to hear and know them no matter how painful you think they may be. I already said that introspection can be uncomfortable, but so can living a bland life while others around you are thriving in abundance.

We do uncomfortable things almost every day of our lives. Sometimes they're even scary things we need to do, but we do them because they're part of living a physical life. Believe me when I say the discomfort and work will be more rewarding than anything else you have ever done. I'll share another trick on how to dive deep into your psyche and EMM in just a moment.

The second R is for *replace*. Take those negative, maladaptive beliefs you discovered you've been harboring and replace them with positive beliefs. That may seem difficult, but it becomes easier with practice. One of my strongest EMM beliefs that formed because of all the abuse I went through was "I'm not good enough." For most of my adult life, that belief was hidden until I did the work I'm sharing with you now. As soon as I finally heard little Vincent say, "You're not good enough," I was able to replace that with this: "Of course, I'm good enough. Look at all I have done and accomplished so far."

Little Vincent's Environment-Made Mind belief stopped me from a lot of things I wanted to do. I got control of that voice though. However, since the scars of my past are so deeply ingrained within, even today I have to pay attention for that inner voice because, if I don't, it will take over again and sabotage all the dreams I still wish to fulfill. As I said before, all injuries cause scars and most of them may never go away. The deeper the injury, the deeper the scar. But you don't have to enflame them and give life to them again either.

The third R stands for *reinforce*. You want to constantly reinforce those new positive beliefs no matter what happens in your life. Maybe you do make a mistake or do something you weren't intending to do that caused a problem. By way of the subconscious automatic mind, that old EMM belief may want to sneak its way back into your conscious mind, but if you're on top of your game, reinforce the positive belief as quickly as you can with something like I say, "Oh, wow. That was a dopey thing I did. Okay, but I can fix that. I'm pretty capable of taking care of anything I need to." Do you know how much better that feels?

And I'm not saying you're not going to mess things up from time to time after you do this work. Since we're living in a physical world, shit will happen. Don't deny when you make a lower choice or mistake. Admit it. Face it. Own it because that's what keeps you from suppressing it. You know how many times I've laughed at myself for some of the stupid things I've done? And as I'm getting older, more of those experiences are happening. However, that doesn't mean I have to be down on myself or aggravate my EMMs. That just means I continue to reinforce all the good things I have to say and believe about myself. And the more you do this work, the more wonderful attitudes and truths arise about yourself. You're a magnificent and divine being. The truth about who you are will surely fill your heart as you let it and stop stopping yourself.

Here's another magic trick that is variation of the Three R System. This one I call the Three A System. Apparently, I like letters. This is another simple method to help you always keep on top of the scars. To make this technique work for you, you have to regard your EMM now as your inner little child.

We're going back to inner child work. We should have never left it. Experts in the fields of psychology and psychiatry agree that the inner child needs to be healed to truly evolve and grow as individuals. Humanist psychologist Carl Rogers said if you remove all the social constraints from humans, they would naturally move in a forward direction. In other words, if we removed all those Environment-Made Mind beliefs that were imposed on us in our youth, we would fulfill our passions and dreams. We're also going to bypass your AMM with this system and go directly into the EMM.

The first A stands for **aware**. Always be aware of and give attention to any negative feeling, thought, or behavior you have. That includes any doubts, fears, or worries. Stop for a moment as soon as one occurs and give it attention. Of course, that means you need to pay more attention to your thoughts, feelings, and behaviors. In the psychology arena, that is called metacognition. In the metaphysical arena, that is called mindfulness. Either way, pay attention and be aware of these thoughts, feelings, and behaviors, and as soon as one is negative in any way, even if it hints of negativity, stop and be aware of it. Then go on to the second A.

The second A is for **acknowledge**. You must acknowledge where that negative thought, feeling, or behavior originated. Remember I told you every negative feeling comes from your EMM? Well, that means it's coming from the little you inside. Adults aren't negative or fearful. They don't fight or lash out at others. They discuss and debate reasonably. They aren't afraid to take chances or risks. Children, however, are negative, fearful, and doubtful, and sometimes they lash out and have uncontrollable emotions.

Every time you get upset, other than from something righteous, an EMM button was pushed. For example, when you're at the market and you get upset because the cashier is taking her time with the customer in front of you and not acknowledging you're in line waiting for her, maybe you think, "What am I, chopped liver here? Come on already." Even getting upset waiting in a line can come from little you.

When you assume someone isn't caring about you because of their lack of attention, that's not an assumption you can make. Maybe the cashier is just overly friendly, but you went to the negative idea because she pushed a button from when you were a kid and your family may not have paid attention to you and you felt you didn't matter. That cashier not attending to you right away reignited that pain almost instantaneously, and you became upset with her.

Your AMM came up with the defense that the cashier was being thoughtless when all the time you felt worthless. So stop. Be aware (the first A) that you have become upset. Acknowledge (the second A) the upset feeling is coming from little you.

The third and most important A is for **affirm**. You must always end this process by affirming the truth for the little you. Adult you must tell little you the opposite of what you're feeling. In the case of this example, you would affirm for little you that it's just not true that you don't matter. "The cashier doesn't even know you, so why would she intentionally ignore you? You're a wonderful kid that everyone can care about and love."

As silly as this dialogue may sound, affirmations like this are vital to retrain your subconscious mind. That's the part of you that automatically goes to places without warning. You must retrain that mind, then, to stop your buttons from being automatically pushed.

You must adhere to the Three A System and the Three R System persistently. No matter how old you are, you have a lot of habits to break. Building self-belief and love takes practice. It really is a matter of retraining your inner child. Just as children do, adults can become belligerent and have temper tantrums. They act out and whine. Staying in touch with your inner child will help you grab hold of the outcome of your life. If you commit to this work and practice these techniques methodically, within a short time you will know immediately when your inner little child is speaking. As soon as you do, you will be able to counter your negative "I'm not" before it causes damage. If not, the little you will keep manifesting what you don't want and sabotaging what you do want. You'll never get a chance to believe in yourself if little you is allowed to remain in control.

I'm sixty-six years old as I'm writing this book. I shared what I experienced mercilessly during my youth. Not only have I been working in the fields of metaphysics, spirituality, and psychology for almost forty years, but I also have been using those fields to work on myself. Though I never felt the need to go for formal therapy because I had the best kind with all the Earthly and spiritual guidance I received along the way, I'm fervently dedicated to listening for little Vincent so I can embrace, love, and re-parent that little boy who never deserved to be treated the way he was. He was such a good kid who loved everyone even while he was being tormented. He was also talented and gifted with wonderful artistic, singing, acting, and dancing abilities that brought joy to his family and many audiences. He was *always* good enough and lovable, and I remind him of this as often as I can. He is the reason I am who I am today, and I love who I am today. Do you love who you are today? You can.

Another effective way to stay in touch with little you is to get yourself a coloring book and color every day. New, amazing coloring books are everywhere now. Though they've been created mostly for meditation and stress reduction practices, coloring has several benefits. First, it pulls you into your right brain, which controls creativity, nurturing, intuition, and emotions. You want to be in that side of your brain as much as possible. Your thinking left brain helped to create your AMM.

Coloring also entices out your inner child, which is why I want you to get a children's coloring book, not an adult one. Maybe a Disney Princess or Marvel Super-hero coloring book would be the best. When you color, invite your inner child to join you. You'll know this technique has worked by either an inner voice actually talking with you or by spontaneous memories of your youth arising when you least expect them. As silly as it sounds, coloring is extremely beneficial in this work. If you don't believe me, try it out for a week and see what happens.

I've told almost all my clients to start coloring, including the guys. Many either wrote me later or shared with me during another reading some of the communications they heard and the experiences they had after they started. Some had spontaneous memories come up during a normal day of events that occurred during their childhoods they didn't remember. Inevitably, those memories had a direct correlation to some of their current issues, and, once they gave attention to those memories, their current issues resolved.

Others had visions of themselves as children reenacting events or circumstances that caused them some form of hurt. Once they visualized those events, they immediately understood how they were connected to current blocks or fears. Following my strategies, they were able to heal those blocks and fears. Then, many heard their inner child actually speak to them, telling them directly what was hurting them. Once hearing those hurts, the adult self-reinforced and affirmed the truths of their inner child's worth, lovability, and magnificence.

All my clients who've done this coloring exercise and the next one I'm going to give you said that they were shocked by what their inner child revealed to them. They had no idea they had suppressed and repressed such negative self-beliefs. They also said they were completely surprised by how fast and effectively my systems worked for them. Remember, God helps those who help themselves. Well, this is the help God was talking about.

This next tool is one of the most powerful ones, and I can't take credit for it. I learned it during a meditation class my wife and I took at our spiritual center. It's called the personification meditation. Although it's called a meditation, you do it with your eyes open so you can write. It's considered an awake meditation because, though your eyes are open and you're writing, you'll still be bypassing your left-brain thinking.

Grab a writing pad and pen or pencil and go to a quiet undisturbed place in your home or wherever you are. This time is yours, so make sure you won't have any distractions. Sit in a chair or on the floor with the pen and pad in your lap. Do this wherever you can be comfortable or where you do your normal meditation routine if you have one.

Close your eyes and briefly focus on the idea that you are going to have a conversation with little you. Tell yourself inwardly that you wish to talk with little you. Use your name to be sure it's personal. Focus gently on that intention for about five to ten minutes. If your mind wanders, just bring it back by saying something like, "Shhhh. This is my time with little (your name). I'm going to talk with little (your name)."

After five or ten minutes, open your eyes and pick up your pad and pen quietly. Then, it's as if you're writing a script for a movie or play. Go over into the left column of your pad and write the character's name, "Big (your name)." That is adult you. Then write a sentence to little you—something like, "Little Vincent, are you there?" When you're done writing that sentence, go back to the left column and under your first line, write the character's name, "Little (your name)." That is your inner child. Now write whatever comes to mind that little you wants to say. Maybe, "Yes, I'm here." Once little you finishes writing, go back to the left column, write your big you name and continue another sentence to little you. Go back and forth with a dialogue until you feel you're done.

Don't read what you're writing yet. Don't judge what you're writing. Don't say to yourself, "Oh, I'm making this all up." It doesn't matter even if you think this is all bullshit. You're writing it for a reason. When you first start this exercise, you may get out only four lines, you may get out four pages. Once you feel you are done writing, then you can go back and read what you wrote. I have included an example here so you can visualize what I'm telling you to do.

**Example of Personification Meditation.**

If you do this practice often, you *will* be shocked with the results. The personification meditation is more effective than journaling. Now, one thing I want to warn you about with any of these exercises is that you may relive unpleasant, painful memories and become emotional. However, understand something important. You can never relive an *emotion*. You can only create a new thought for the memory that will create a new emotion. Once the event, whatever it was, and your initial emotion caused by it was felt, the emotion is gone. If you start getting upset from the memories that little you is sharing, you're causing that with new negative thoughts.

I do want you to be cautious as you do the coloring and personification work. Don't re-upset yourself or little you will go back into hiding again. Remember, your Adult-Made Mind wants to protect you from pain. For example, let's say during the writing little you says she or he was really hurt by your brother hitting you one day. Don't turn around and think or say something that gets you pissed at your brother like, "That stupid bastard! I can't believe he hit me like that." That certainly will cause you to get angry all over again.

Instead, be as a good parent would be to little you with any painful words little you shares. Be willing to listen and be gentle and compassionate and caring because it will probably be the first time little you will have experienced love in that way in a long time if at all. Say something like, "I'm so sorry you were hurt, honey. That must have really upset you. Your brother was probably having a real bad day. It wasn't your fault. And look at how good you are today. You don't go around hurting anyone. I love you."

Sounds corny? Well, do you think "I'm a real piece of shit! I can't believe I fucked up again" is a better thing to say to or about yourself? Get over feeling uncomfortable saying warm, fuzzy, touchy-feely stuff to yourself. And that goes for both men and women. We don't say anywhere near enough warm, fuzzy things to ourselves. But we will be the first to criticize ourselves before anyone else does.

Do you want to stop stopping yourself? Then you need to believe and say a hell of a lot of wonderful things about yourself. How would you compliment God? Well, you're God's child. Would you say, "Hey, God, you're a really beautiful and loving spirit, but your kid is a real piece of crap"?

Always reinforce the positive for little you. You have to retrain your subconscious mind and replace your Environment-Made Mind beliefs. Let me speak a little about affirmations since we're broaching that subject. I love affirmations. Louise Hay created an entire empire, Hay House Publishing, based on affirmations. In fact, she cured herself from stage-four breast cancer when she was in her sixties by adding daily affirmations with her other treatments. However, affirmations, touchy-feely words, New Age and New Thought philosophies, or the like all come with a vital caveat that gets over-looked by many, including luminaries, spiritual leaders and teachers, and metaphysical practitioners. I'll explain the caveat by giving an illustration.

I want you to visualize a large whiteboard in your mind's eye. You can do this with your eyes open or closed. It's not an exercise. It's just a point I'm making. On that whiteboard, I want you to write every negative feeling and thought you might have in your Environment-Made Mind. Any negative experience you had or also caused. See them all written down on the board. Got it? Make some up if your Adult-Made Mind is hiding them well.

Okay, now let's say you already read about the power of affirmations, and you attended some New Thought spiritual center or watched an inspirational movie, or you received online memes and graphics that have all these beautiful quotes and sayings and points about us as spiritual beings.

Then, see all those positive words and thoughts as pretty pictures or keep them as words, and now paste them all over your whiteboard you have with all the negative stuff on it. Go ahead. Paste them everywhere so you no longer see any of the crappy things. What you're left with is something like a vision board completely covered with wonderful words, ideas, affirmations, and pretty pictures. Nice, right? Have you changed anything? Have you replaced the negative words and feelings? No, you haven't. You haven't changed one thing. You just covered them up. You just did consciously what your AMM does unconsciously. Yet this is what is mostly taught in your most advanced spiritual writings, classes, books, and centers.

The whole New Thought movement is based on having a "new thought" to create a new outcome for your life. It's not that I disagree. It's that they are not teaching the complete process necessary to create a new life, a more fulfilling one, an abundant one. You *must* replace and rid yourself of what you put on the whiteboard first before you can take on new and prettier beliefs and concepts. Remember, you may have been trying to do just that when you ended up saying, "God, it's not working!" Those negative feelings and beliefs will pierce right through all the pretty ones you pasted over them.

This whiteboard visualization is another way of demonstrating to you the layers and workings of your EMM and AMM. Your EMM is your whiteboard with all the negative stuff you put on it, and your AMM beliefs are all the pretty words and pictures you used to cover your whiteboard. It takes all the work I have presented in this book to clear the whiteboard and your EMM.

And you don't have to wipe the whiteboard completely clean or empty your Environment-Made Mind completely before adding higher consciousness understandings. You have to start the process, and the Universe, as I said, will help you complete it with validations and reinforcing messages and signs that you're on the right path and journey.

Believing in yourself becomes easier once you have faced your AMM and EMM. For those of you who have a fairly good life with friends, a partner, kids, a well-paying job, no illnesses, and maybe enough money to go on vacation but who have never achieved more than a modest life, it may be easier for you to find reasons to gain self-belief. You can review all you have accomplished and know it was all through your manifesting.

For those of you who are impoverished and just barely surviving or who come from a tormented background even worse than mine, you may have a much more difficult time finding better beliefs to replace the bad ones and any reason to believe in yourself. But there's still hope. There's nothing on this Earth that makes you worthy, deserving, or even lovable. And there's no one human who does that either, including your parents or lovers. Remember, you're innately magnificent because you're divine. You were made that way upon your creation. That is all you truly need to believe.

I recommend several books you can read to keep the process going. One such book is called *Homecoming: Reclaiming & Championing Your Inner Child* by John Bradshaw. Bradshaw suggests that your inner child influences most of your adult life, which is exactly what

I have said about your EMM. He also claims that you need to re-parent yourself and give everything to little you that you might not have received growing up. You need to fulfill your own emotional needs, in other words. In his work with clients, he actually makes them purchase Teddy bears and dolls to personify as their inner child. I, too, had to intensely do this exact work, which is what led me to all my research and studies and why I know how well this works. If you go to my website (vincentgenna.com), there are several more books I list under the Resources tab that can also help.

Become involved in practices that make you feel good about yourself and eliminate those that don't. Let the adult you take control. It's difficult to believe in yourself if you keep making bad choices or being inconsiderate of others. Just focus on what we all know to be God or moral values. You can't go wrong making choices guided by those. Forgive all the people you think you need to forgive, including yourself, and release all your angers and frustrations, including those directed toward yourself. How do you get to believe you're divine by holding onto anger and lack of forgiveness? Positive self-talk every day and all day is necessary to combat the negative automatic self-talk you do.

Whatever you do, stop making fear-based choices. That again is negative and influenced by little you. As Yoda from the movie saga *Star Wars* said, you must face your fears. Facing them will resolve them. Unconsciously, you may believe within your EMM that you're not strong enough to handle certain situations, so you fear them. Face your fears and admit them; then just like all parents tell their children, tell little you there's nothing to be afraid of. I'm not talking about facing your fears of snakes and spiders or jumping out of planes. We can all still live quite fulfilled not ever getting over those unless, of course, you wish to move to Arizona or join the Air Force.

Also, stop using limiting sayings, prayers, quotes, and affirmations that sound good but serve no benefit in reminding you how unlimited you are. For example, I want to share with you an old prayer that has worked for decades for many people to encourage and help them cope with the challenges of life. As I said before, coping skills teach you how to survive, not how to thrive. I believe that prayer, although it seemed to work during the time it was needed, has regrettably disempowered people by making them believe they are limited.

Historians aren't totally certain of who wrote this prayer. For the longest time, St. Francis of Assisi got the credit while others claimed the American theologian Reinhold Niebuhr (1892–1971) wrote it. Whoever wrote it, it's one of the most famous prayers, which is even used in the Alcoholics Anonymous treatment program:

> *"God, grant me the serenity to accept the things I*
> *cannot change, the courage to change the things*
> *I can, and the wisdom to know the difference."*

The things I cannot change—really? That is so limiting of our understanding of who we really are. That is a total Adult-Made Mind defense to counter the feelings of "I'm not good enough" or "I'm not lovable." How many people have you ever heard say in defeat, "I can't change this," "I can't change him," "I can't change her," "I can't change who I am," "I can't change my circumstances," and so on. With this understanding, Paula, whom I wrote about earlier, and thousands of others I've worked with would have never tried to save or help their marriages, relationships, and themselves.

We can change and influence *everything*. We are co-creators even within our human form. There's a plethora of evidence proving that claim. Tell the people who totally cured themselves of stage-four cancer that they couldn't change everything after all their doctors told them there was no cure and they were terminal.

So, I rewrote "The Serenity Prayer" and renamed it "The Empowerment Prayer":

> *"God, grant me the conviction to believe there is noth-*
> *ing I cannot change, the courage to change all I want,*
> *and the wisdom to know what's best left the way it is."*

You see, it's not that we can't change everything. There are some things, like our pasts, that we shouldn't change. We need to learn to use our pasts to grow, not get rid of them or change them no matter how painful they were.

Copy my prayer denoting me as the author and place it in your home or work where you can see, read, and say it out lout as often as possible. Remember what I have told you here, and every time you're tempted to say, "I can't change—," come back to the prayer and know that you can. You can change all you want.

This work isn't easy because it takes commitment to yourself and constant vigilance. No matter how old I am, little Vincent still rears his head every so often after all these years and all I have accomplished. My ingrained "I'm not" is "I'm not good enough." Little Vincent is still in there wounded, but my self-belief became strong enough to hear and control him. It took some time, but it was so worth it.

One of the other best ways to do this work is with support. Turn to family members, your partner, friends, work associates, or anyone you know who would benefit from this work and ask him, her, or them to join you on this journey. Believe me when I say no one you ask should say, "I'm not interested," because everyone can afford to love and believe in themselves more than they currently do. Everyone here, especially during this time, can afford to manifest more of what they want.

Come to my "The Secret That's Holding You Back" dedicated and private Facebook group and join in the conversation with others who've read this book and are doing the work. Share with them as they share with you their successes and challenges. We're here together on this planet to experience unity. We're here together to thrive and evolve, and we can help each other do that. I know it sounds trite to say, but there is power in numbers. Attend one of my in-person or online events for that proof and experience the power of all those participating. It's mind-blowing and totally awe-inspiring.

Once again, here is the most important message you can say to yourself as often as you can that will help give you the motivation you need. It did for me. Let it be the first thing you say when you wake up in the morning and the last thing you say before falling asleep at night. It never gets old or weak. It becomes more and more empowering: "I love myself so much I'm going to do whatever I need to do to experience my greatest existence here on Earth because I deserve it."

If you want, you can even add a little native New Yorker attitude at the end: "because I deserve it, *damn it!*"

You can do this. After all, if you're reading this book, you've already come a long way in opening your mind to new possibilities and the desire to flourish and ascend to the highest consciousness you can. Don't stop. Walk this talk. Do it every day. Commit to yourself to do it because you are worth it, damn it!

I leave you with this. From my heart and soul, I believe in you, especially if you can't believe in yourself. I have to. You are my sister. You are my brother. You are my them. You are my ze. And if this life is not going to work for you, it's not going to work for me either nor for any of us. After all, we are one family created from the same divine force. Believe it or not, we fall together, and we stand together. I choose to believe it will work for all of us, not just some of us. I'm no more special than you.

I just awakened the wisdom within me that we all have, and I only hope some of what you read here resonated with you. And even if I leave this Earth before you, I will still be here with you to guide and help you. I totally get it when Jesus said after he ascended that he would be with us until the end of eternity. When you love yourself, you are capable of loving others so deeply. The *true* words Jesus said at his last supper, before the Council of Nicaea bastardized them in about AD 535, were that the two greatest commandments were to love the God within you with all your heart and all your might, and, then as you love yourself in that way, you will be able to love your neighbor the same.

I wish for you that all your dreams, your passions, and your desires are fulfilled in this life. I wish for you abundant unconditional love for yourself and unconditional belief in yourself. You are all you seek, and, most of all, you are love. See all of who you are, your Godness, your gifts, and talents through my eyes. Then go do what you need to do to see that all through your own. I love you. Namaste. Peace.

# Acknowledgments

Behold, how good and how pleasant it is
For brethren to dwell together in unity!
Psalms 133:1 (King James Version)

*T*hat is such an important and vital under-standing that Leonard Bernstein wrote a song to that psalm and included it in his trilogy called *The Chichester Psalms*. It's a most beautiful piece of work that I have had the joy of singing with the All State Choir at the Eastman School of Music in Rochester, New York, and with famous opera singers as soloists, the New York Symphony, and a renowned conductor.

I bring this up here because unity among brethren does more than bring joy. Unity brings support, help, and, of course, love. This book is a result of the unity of the many people who inspired, supported, taught, and helped me become who I am today with all the blessings I possess, and I must acknowledge them for all they gave. There are far more than I can list, for everyone I have ever met has influenced my life in some way. But those listed here had an effect on this book.

If not for Dennis S, I would not even possess the gifts and wisdom I have today. It was he, my original enemy turned dear friend, who inspired my overwhelming passion to help when he was experiencing his greatest turmoil. My first unselfish cry to God to give me the abilities to help him and others like him transformed my life and my family's lives forever. Dennis joyfully became my first spiritual mentee.

I'd be remiss if I didn't acknowledge the first psychic who began my journey and spiritual awakening: Doris from Queens, New York. At my first psychic party, she told me that the soul of Jesus was around me and that I was to become a spiritual teacher. If it weren't for her messages and genuine words of pride and love for me, along with that supernatural follow-up trancing evening, I would have never started my quest to learn all about the purpose and meaning of the messages and my role in it all.

I could never say enough about my dearest friends, Bonnie and her first husband, Pat, who transitioned too young at thirty-three years old. Pat and Bonnie attended that psychic party, and Pat was skeptical about it all. However, after profound paranormal things started occurring with me, Pat became quite curious and insisted I share everything that was happening and all the insights that were now filling my mind and lips.

Pat and Bonnie hosted many evenings of talk and new psychic trancing and communication that lasted until six o'clock in the morning. Our toddlers, one each, would lie sleeping on the floor with us so the talks could continue uninterrupted. We were all so dedicated to this curious awakening that was unfolding. In fact, after we moved to New Jersey, Pat and Bonnie soon moved there as well, and we continued our evening-to-sunrise talks. I truly believe that was providence because if it weren't for their unwavering support, I could have never continued my pursuit of my new supernatural calling. I love them dearly for the blessings they helped me achieve.

Jason T, JJ W, Jason J, Scott H, Nate H-C, and Chris K were all my earliest clients who became my friends and who believed in me and always wanted me to share my wisdom and insight with each of them. They also patiently listened to my soapbox lectures and guidance that were continuously expanding. If not for them, I wouldn't have gained the necessary knowledge and passion to write this book. I am eternally grateful for them all. And though Nate left this physical world too early, I know he watches over me to see and support my progress.

I have to acknowledge our children, Jacob and Kimberly, for their endearing support and tolerance since they were young kids. Jake was two-and-a-half years old when this all started for me, and Kimberly came in almost seven years later. They bore all my early learning experiences and the bizarre paranormal events I was going through and sharing. When they were older, they never knew whether to have a family intervention because of my wild psychic and medium-ship claims, especially after I started talking psychically with animals, or to just walk around thinking they have a crazy father. They actually chose to unconditionally love, support, and be proud of the work I do.

I, at least, was a resource for Jacob and his wife, Marissa, when their firstborn had his own psychic and medium experiences at three-and-a-half years old. In fact, Jacob, Marissa, Kimberly, and her husband, Michael, now refer their friends and acquaintances to me. And I must throw in that our grandchildren, Noah, Caleb, and Lyla, have no problem bragging to their peers and teachers that their poppy is a psychic medium. Of course, their peers always respond, "What the hell is that?" Their teachers, on the other hand, say very curiously, "OOOO! That's interesting."

For the longest time in my latter years, I myself felt blocked and needed an outside source to help me understand how I was getting in my way of achieving my highest dreams. Turning to God for direction, providence stepped in again. It turned out my wife, Eileen, wanted to become part of a spiritual community, and, as synchronicity would have it, we happened to be attending a monthly event at Spiritual Frontiers Fellowship (SFF), a Raleigh metaphysical educational organization, and the guest speaker for the evening was Rev. Denise Schubert from the Triangle Center for Spiritual Living in Raleigh, North Carolina. We fell in love with her and her message right away. She kept quoting and speaking concepts that I was teaching, and Eileen and I took that as a sign to become members of Reverend Denise's beautiful community. Both Reverend Denise and the woman who became her assistant minister, Rev. Dusty Ripplemeyer, fed us the most important spiritual nourishment that opened the floodgates to our new prosperity. Both ministers continually reinforced, to me, the need to let go and trust who I already was. The musical *Wicked* has an amazingly beautiful song in it called "For Good," which has some of the most profound lyrics that I rightly believe. Go listen to the full song and lyrics, but the best line from the song that I hold true about these ministers is that knowing them, I have been changed. They have both become two of our dearest friends and soul sisters and part of our spiritual tribe.

To my editors, Lisa Fugard and Sandra Wendel, I extend much gratitude. Lisa was the editor I worked with for my first draft of this book, and we spent a long time getting it together. She never lost her belief in my work and encouraged me all the way from the time we met to the time we completed my first draft. Her talent and passion for writing helped to shape my ideas and words.

Sandra is my publisher's editor, and she pushed and challenged me to go the deepest I could and to write as I speak, for that is my forte.

I wouldn't have been able to start or complete this book without the generosity and support of our dear friends Marty and Carol S. They so lovingly offered their beautiful beach house as a retreat for me to seclude myself from life's distractions so I could concentrate on this book. The warmth of their house and serenity of the beach and ocean inspired me creatively.

And last, and the most important acknowledgment I must make is the hardest for me to write because I can never get through thinking about this person without welling up with tears. There is a verse in the Bible that goes like this: "I looked for someone among them who would build up the wall and stand before me in the gap on behalf of the land so I would not have to destroy it, but I found no one." Ezekiel 22:30 (The New International Version)

The interpretation I take from this is God was looking for someone who believed enough in his or her brothers and sisters to stand for them, support them. God couldn't find any then, but I did. At seventeen years old, I met Eileen, who became the first person to totally believe in me and love me unconditionally with all my idiosyncrasies.

From the beginning, she saw my true personality and character, my talents and gifts, my values and morals, and most of all my Godness. She was 100 percent supportive of my career as a performer and attended every show I did, sitting in the front row every time. She even left her entire family to move with me to California after we got married. And when I wanted to return to New York to pursue Broadway, she said, "Let's go for it," as if it were her idea too.

During our hardest times and struggles, her love and belief in me never waned. Then after having a child and living in Levittown, New York, where all the fantastic paranormal stuff happened to me, she still stood by my side, believing that I had come into a new and special mission that was going to take our family on an exciting journey.

While having two children in school and being the primary income provider, Eileen sent me back to school full-time to obtain my degrees. For seven years, she was the primary support for our family.

She has *never* doubted me and my abilities nor my choices. And whenever I was or am at my weakest, she stands in that gap in the wall for me, reminding me of my passions and abilities and purpose. Even with her own full-time position as a senior vice president for the company where she works, she still takes the time to be my business manager and takes part in all my events. In fact, she has her own reception line at the end of all my events, so the audiences have a chance to talk with her as well.

Eileen and I will have been together for forty-nine years by the time this book is published and married for almost forty-four years. She is the reason I was even able to write this book. She believes in it and cleared all the time I needed to complete it from our schedule and activities. I dedicate this book to my best friend, my companion, my collaborator, my soul mate, my lover, Eileen. Thank you for always seeing the God in me and in the work I do. I love you everlastingly.

# About the Author

$\mathcal{A}$s a young adult, Vincent Genna suddenly found himself blessed with keen psychic abilities—a gift that came with tremendous responsibility. Each time he works with clients, he never forgets that he holds their soul in his hands.

For almost four decades, Vincent has helped thousands of people around the world heal, unlock, and release their passions and purpose, and transform their lives through his inspiring and enlightening radio and television interviews, dynamic and powerful keynote presentations, workshops, training classes, and private sessions. Relatable, deeply compassionate, humorous, and a gifted mystic healer, Vincent offers his clients the opportunity for deep emotional healing and radical spiritual awakening and the key to make everything they attempt work.

For Vincent, helping his clients process and use otherworldly messages is as important as divining those messages for them. To this end, Vincent pursued and added a set of key educational credentials to his skill set as a psychic by earning a BA in psychology and a master's in social work. He is also a practiced hospice clinical social worker, a profession that allowed him the privilege of helping more than 500 patients peacefully transition through their dying process while comforting and supporting their families and friends.

Having been a psychotherapist, and as a psychic medium, Vincent is compelled and deeply committed to continually fine-tuning his skills as a medium. He considers both his innate and academic abilities to be instruments requiring deep respect and ongoing care. That commitment has led Vincent to continuing advanced psychic and medium work and training with the world's foremost medium experts, including James Van Praagh and Europe's renowned experts, Tony Stockwell, Lynn Probert, and Paul Jacobs as well as studying at The Arthur Findlay College (for the advancement of spiritualism and psychic sciences) in England.

Beloved by the media, Vincent is a regular guest on major ABC, CBS, NBC, and affiliate network television and radio shows around the country and has also been a featured guest on Gaia's *Beyond Belief*, *World News Today*, and *Good Morning America*. Radio loves Vincent as well with his numerous regular interviews on national and international power radio networks and shows such as *Coast-to-Coast AM with George Noory*, iHeart Radio, and Sirius XM. Popular YouTube channels such as those of Logan Paul and Michael Sandler and spiritual education online sites like The Shift Network have featured interviews with Vincent.

He has also presented workshops and programs at many spiritual centers and organizations across the country, including the Institute of Noetic Sciences, International Association of Near-Death Studies, Afterlife Research and Education Institute, Infinity Foundation, Kripalu Center for Yoga & Health, Center for Spiritual Living, and Unity.

Not only is he beloved on US television, but the UK also loves Vincent. Sky Network, one of the largest broadcast networks in the UK, featured Vincent as a regular guest on one of its TV shows, and Lion TV did a special on Vincent's gift for communicating with animals.

Vincent's range of experiences with humans, animals, and spirits has been beyond compare, but now his psychic communication skills have even gone outside this universe into the other galaxies. For the past few years, Vincent has been communicating with an intergalactic council of extraterrestrial beings in spirit who contacted him first. They have been sharing indepth information about their Earthly visits in hopes that Vincent will share the truth and dispel the fallacies and falsehoods about UFOs, aliens, and human abductions. Since then, Vincent has become involved with renowned and expert ufologists and MUFON (Mutual UFO Network) representatives.

Everyone who experiences a Vincent Genna event or session goes home enlightened, energized, and empowered—emotionally prepared to unlock and release their passions and purposes, and possessing the key to achieving their life goals and fulfilling their dreams.